ANIMAL ARCHITECTS

ANIMAL ARCHITECTS

How Animals Weave, Tunnel, and Build
Their Remarkable Homes

Wanda Shipman

Illustrations by Marna Grove

STACKPOLE
BOOKS

Published by
STACKPOLE BOOKS
5067 Ritter Road
Mechanicsburg, PA 17055

Printed in the United States of America

10 9 8 7 6 5 4 3 2 1

First edition

Cover design by Tracy Patterson
Cover illustration by Marna Grove

Library of Congress Cataloging-in-Publication Data

Shipman, Wanda.
    Animal architects : how animals weave, tunnel, and build their
remarkable homes / Wanda Shipman ; illustrations by Marna Grove. —
1st ed.
        p.   cm.
    Includes bibliographical references (p.   ) and index.
    ISBN 0-8117-2404-2
    1. Animals—Habitations.   I. Title.
QL756.S52   1994
591.56'4—dc20   93-36014
                                                                          CIP

*To Bert
(and the rest of the clan: Boo,
Jasper, Woody, Rufus, Missy, and Gomez)*

CONTENTS

PREFACE

A LOVE OF THE NATURAL WORLD CAN BE CULTIVATED AT ANY TIME and in any season. No particular knowledge or tools are needed to appreciate the wonders of plant and animal life. I believe that people naturally become more attuned to wildlife as they begin to see their own most primal needs for shelter, food, and protection for their young played out need for need in the world outside their homes and offices.

Animals are much more than the instinct-driven automatons that science for centuries held them to be. Evidence abounds of animals improvising and adapting to new situations. Individuals of a given species often possess distinct personalities, interests, and proclivities. Animals are capable of caring for and responding to the needs of their mates and offspring as deeply as any human. This is the understanding that will draw us more deeply into the world that parallels our own in so many fascinating ways. This also may be the deeper sort of "knowing" that we must acquire if we want to protect and preserve those who also make their homes in our neighborhoods.

ONE

Blueprints for Survival

HE EARLIEST BUILDING DESIGNS USED BY OUR ANCESTORS actually survive today in the remarkable shelters that animals build to withstand the elements and to protect their young. The first human building forms were the stone pile (cairn) and the earthen mound (barrow or tumulus). These rudimentary architectural designs can be seen in the rounded contours of Byzantine domes and in the arches of the Roman aqueducts. Cairns and barrows form the basic architectural contours of the greatest pyramids as well as the simplest medieval mud hut. The same designs can also be seen in the beaver lodge, the groundhog's earthen mound, and the hill of an ant colony.

An animal's shelter is often much more complex than its simple exterior ever reveals. The warrenlike subterranean chambers and passages of the Roman catacombs are identical in conception, if not in scope, to the meandering underground tunnel systems excavated by many burrowing animals. The hollow cells of wax surrounding the queen bee in a honeybee's hive are akin to early religious structures in which a nucleus chamber built for a deity was encircled by a group of individual chambers called *cella*. Supporting columns of earth are sometimes found inside the surface mounds of larger anthills. The crossed structural members of Buckminster Fuller's remarkable geodesic domes or the diamond-shaped iron ribs of the Eiffel

1

Tower are similar in both appearance and function to the silken grid of the orb spider's web.

A building material is either structural or nonstructural, load-bearing or non-load-bearing. A material either works to hold a building together under pressure or is used to provide warmth, decoration, camouflage, or weatherproofing. Structural building materials withstand one or two kinds of stress—compression or tension. Roughly speaking, a material used under compression tends to be hard, dense, and inflexible; it is reduced in size by the weight resting upon it. A material that is used under tension is generally lighter and more elastic and is stretched and pulled out of shape by the weight hanging from it.

Many materials used under compression such as stone, concrete, lumber, and brick, often break under tension, while elastic materials such as plant fibers and silk are useless under compression. Materials of great tensile strength such as steel and silk can withstand a tremendous amount of pressure without snapping or distorting. Heavy materials such as brick and concrete often fail by shearing or buckling under their own weight, while elastic materials fail when they are stressed beyond their limits to rebound to their normal contours. Given all of these limitations, the quest for the ideal building material can take centuries.

The early cathedrals, for example, were made of huge stones and bricks, yet most of these massive structures have since crumbled from the very weight of the building materials themselves. It was not until the nineteenth century that architects discovered that iron and steel were both lightweight and strong and much easier to use in churches, office buildings, towers, and bridges.

Animals build their homes of durable, high-tensile materials. Wood and plant fibers share the merits and strengths of compression *and* tension. Glass and wood are both hard materials, but while glass easily shatters completely under too much pressure, wood will crack without falling apart. In this sense wood is hard yet pliable. It can bear great loads without failing.

This is why nearly all of our homes are still framed in wood, which is light enough to lift and work with, flexible enough to withstand high winds, and strong enough to bear a great deal of weight.

Wood, bark, plant stems, leaves, grass, and other natural fibers contain cellulose, a substance that gives them great strength, weather-resistance, and pliability. These organic materials are cheap and plentiful and can handle the strains of both compression and tension. Other organic materials make equally strong binders. When mixed with saliva, mud and grass become as tough and weather-resistant as the best mortars. The long *bast* fibers of plant stems can have the strength of nylon cord. The silk of spiderwebs and insect cocoons, when comparably stressed by wind, rain, and the weight of insects, has been rated alongside steel for its high flexibility and tensile strength.

Animals select their building materials according to availability, needs, and ease of use. The garden spider can find nothing better for its building needs than the silk it produces within its own body. And only a spider's quick and delicate feet can work with this gossamer substance. Small birds have the dexterity needed to weave their cup nests of mosses, plant down, and shredded plants, and these lightweight fibers are all that are needed to support the eggs and growing chicks. Beavers possess the strength and durability needed to work with heavier building materials like rocks and tree limbs, and burrowers such as groundhogs, bears, and badgers have the sheer digging power to use the earth itself as a building material.

Animals must transport their building supplies back to the home site. Just as the Egyptians floated huge stones down the Nile for their pyramids and monuments, beavers carve canals leading from the water into the woods so they can gather and float tree branches back to the lodge. Birds carry twigs and other nesting-building materials in their beaks and feet. Swallows scoop mud out of the ground and carry it to their nests in their mouths, while eagles lift tree limbs in their talons. Bees carry nectar, the raw material of honey, back to the hive in special honey sacs, and the tiny half-ounce harvest mouse uses grass stems as ladders to reach its woven sleeping bag.

Dead leaves, wool, twigs, moss, feathers, and other fibrous insulating materials add warmth and cushioning to nests and burrows. Camouflage is important even to the welfare of our largest animals. Before entering their hibernation chambers for the winter, bears obscure their den entrances with pine boughs or brush. Some materials seem to be used for aesthetic reasons alone. Many birds "decorate" their nests with colored yarns, snakeskins, and dollar bills. The Spanish architect Antonio Gaudí y Cornet had similar tastes. He embellished his surrealistic Gothic architecture, which reflects the dreamy style of the Art Nouveau period, with real and fantasized shapes from nature, including snails, fish scales, flowers, and bones.

Animals seem to understand that composite materials are often superior for their needs. Many mammals and birds mix mud with grass stems or sand before using it as a mortar or binder. As all carpenters know, a plaster mixed with wood fibers is a good deal stronger and lighter and can take a nail (or twig) without crumbling. Swallows mix mud and saliva to form the walls of their nests, and hornets add saliva to wood fibers to process their paper pulp. Hummingbirds completely "shingle" lichens to their tiny cup nests using insect silk as a binder, strengthening and camouflaging the nest at the same time.

It is the cellulose in wood and plant fibers and the protein in saliva and silk that give these natural building materials their great plasticity and durability. Honeybees use a particularly refined building material for their nests. The wax that honeybees produce for their combs is formulated especially for housing the brood and storing pollen and honey. Honeybees also collect and process from wood fibers a varnishlike substance called *propolis*. Its weatherproofing and binding properties cannot be matched in a laboratory because the honeybees alone possess the necessary additive.

An animal usually chooses its homesite carefully, gauging the energy it will have to expend to collect and transport materials compared with the time and energy it will need to breed, raise its young, and forage for food. The local weather conditions are taken into account as well as the presence of predators. Even future needs are considered. If a growing or extended family will need more space next season, the chosen site must be large enough to allow for expansion. Honeybees and smaller birds frequently "pace out" a likely building site before they begin building to make sure it is large enough.

Animals can be painstaking architects, doing much more than roughing out a hasty shelter for the breeding season. They polish out interior chambers, tunnels, and cells before using them. While the badger often burrows out a slapdash den, bears will invest as much time in choosing and arranging the linings of their hibernation chambers as they do in excavating the den itself. In spring and summer, beavers in a large established colony take the time to fill in and smooth over cracks and crevices in their dams and lodges. They are also able to gauge the pressure of the water flowing through their dams and shore them up as the need arises. The tiny, predatory trapdoor spider weaves a squeak-free silken hinge for the round door to its underground den. The door is so skillfully constructed that it swings shut on its own, sealing off the burrow entrance as firmly as a boat hatch.

Ants, wasps, honeybees, beavers, and polar bears all control the temperature and humidity levels in their nearly air-tight dwellings and use reliable methods to ventilate excess moisture. Ants are experts at building self-regulating environments. Biosphere II, a huge experimental glass-and-steel compound near Tucson, Arizona, is designed to regenerate food, oxygen, and water in a completely sealed environment. Likewise, leaf-cutting ants grow "gardens" of fungus inside the ant hill, handling the exchange of gases, ventilation, lighting, and other conditions needed to produce the food the entire colony depends on.

Just as new and improved building materials are embraced by humans, animals also experiment at times. Birds seem to be the most open-minded innovators, sometimes substituting yarn, human hair, and paper in their nests, and have even used wire and cement in the place of twigs and mud. Beavers are known for using whatever is at hand in their dams and lodges, but many other mammals have been known to line their burrows with discarded clothing and paper. While animals do not change the designs of their dwellings, they do experiment with the materials they use, and if they find something superior to an old material, they continue to use it.

Animals are capable of refining their work over time. Young animals often build sloppy, ill-formed dwellings at first, but their building skills improve as they grow in size and experience. Tiny spiderlings weave awkward little webs immediately after birth, but by adulthood all can spin a perfect web.

Animals may be largely instinct-bound when it comes to their building designs, but we humans are resistant to change as well. Our own architecture has evolved very slowly. It took the Greeks many generations of experimentation to refine the simple post and lintel. New building methods usually gain widespread acceptance only after they have been proven to be superior to the old ways, and often they are accepted only by force. We would still be hoisting massive timbers to build our homes had all the large trees not disappeared during the last century.

Buckminster Fuller, who was an inspiring force for the architect who designed Biosphere II, had a guiding vision that was simple but difficult to sell. He believed that a building should provide much more value than the cost of the materials and energy that went into the making of it. The structural materials should be light and cheap, and as much as possible the building should take advantage of the offerings of the environment. His famous geodesic domes were so constructed that the placement of the extremely lightweight building members gave these structures tremendous strength and space compared with their own weight and cost.

Fuller aimed for beauty as well as function, but his architectural plans were never pursued at the expense of efficiency. His engineering knowledge made it impossible for him to ignore wasted time, materials, and energy when better solutions were possible, and he claimed that a building should succeed as well as nature does in combining form with function. As one of the first proponents of environmental architecture, Buckminster Fuller no doubt appreciated the fact that the proof for many of his landmark building theories existed right in the midst of the animal kingdom.

PART ONE

Anatomical Engineers

T HE ROMAN CATACOMBS WERE CARVED OUT OF TUFA, A SOFT and malleable limestone rock formed by the deposits of hot springs and rivers. The walls of this vast underground network of earthen passages are lined throughout with shallow *loculi*. These tiered niches, carved one above the other like so many mail slots, once held the shrouded bodies of dead Christians whose remains were sealed inside their burial niches with slabs of marble or terra cotta.

The Roman catacombs run from 20 to 60 feet beneath the earth's surface and branch out in a bewildering maze of winding tunnels across nearly 600 acres. Many of the interior passages lead into *cubicula*, special large, circular burial chambers that once held the remains of entire families. The passages of the catacombs bisect one another throughout the system. They connect vertically as well as horizontally, forming a confusing labyrinth that defies above-surface orientation. Dozens of concealed passages lead from the catacombs up to the surface, many of them opening out of the sides of hills near roads and highways.

The diggers who carved out the Roman catacombs were called *fossores*. They carried with them down into the earth nothing more than lamps, simple picks, and baskets to carry out the soft rock removed from the tunnels. They followed no excavation plans. These diggers had to rely upon memory and the sense of touch to tell them the general direction in which they were digging, which was more often than not dictated by the workability of the rock and the presence of air. Many of the passages are stacked one above the other like the *loculi* themselves, separated and supported by only a few feet of earth between each level. Perhaps the most remarkable thing about the Roman catacombs is that nearly two thousand years after the first tunnels were excavated, this dark subterranean warren of passages and chambers remains largely intact.

Earth as home, birth, or burial site is also common to many animals. For our largest group of mammals, the rodents, a life underground is the only safe one. The earth is highly insulating several feet beneath the surface, and a good snow cover will keep burrowers warm throughout the winter. Building within

the ground is largely a matter of removal. Woodchucks, badgers, gophers, and other tunnelers work completely in the dark
and must also find ways to carry out the soil excavated from
their tunnels. The pocket gopher carries dirt out in its cheek
pouches after every inch or so of tunnel that it digs. Badgers
and bears simply hurl the dirt behind them with their powerful
legs, leaving a telltale spray of dirt and rocks or a mound of
earth at the entrance to their burrows and caves.

Virtually every tunneler's burrowing site is marked by an
earthen mound, whether it is the 3-inch-high pile of dirt left by
a chipmunk at the entrance to its tiny burrow or the 4-foot-high
cairn at the face of a grizzly's den. Most smaller animals use
these excavated dirt mounds as convenient perches from which
they can eye the surrounding area for predators, bask in sunny
weather, or look for promising forage.

To be useful and safe, burrows must stay dry and intact.
Burrowing animals always take into account the condition of
the soil and the possibility of flooding. Burrowers work soil that
is just easy enough to dig without crumbling during excavation
but firm enough to withstand constant daily use. Flooding or
collapse would be devastating for the helpless young, which are
always hidden deep within an interior chamber. Most burrow
passages leading to sleeping and breeding chambers are dug on
a slight upslant to ensure good water drainage. And sometimes
these chambers are camouflaged by several dummy passages
that dead-end or loop back around to the main passage.

Smaller and weaker burrowers avoid rocky soil, but badgers
and bears are more than capable of handling large rocks and
tough plant roots. Grizzly bears simply toss big rocks, dead
wood, and other heavy debris aside with their front paws,
sometimes uprooting saplings and other small trees that may be
in the way of their work. Bears often dig their dens directly
beneath a well-matted root system to take advantage of the
strengthened soil, while gophers do the same thing, but mainly
so they can feed on the plant roots from the safety of their
burrows.

Animals actually have a few more digging tools than the
fossores of the Roman catacombs. All burrowing animals have

powerful picklike claws, and almost all of them use their teeth as excavating tools to dig plant roots and grass out of the earth. Even the tiny burrowing purse-web and trapdoor spiders have stronger mandibles and legs than other spiders. But the most skillful burrowers are the rodents. Their bodies are compact, their necks and legs are short and sturdy, and their eyes and ears are small. It is an anatomy that is perfectly suited to drilling through the earth. Some rodents have protective ear and eye coverings, and all have long, sharp incisors that are powered by large skulls and strong jaw muscles.

Constant gnawing on wood, nuts, and other tough vegetation sharpens these perpetually growing incisors. A rodent's teeth not only are efficient digging tools but also make daunting weapons when necessary. A fox foolish enough to squeeze into a woodchuck burrow—especially if there is a nest of young 'chucks inside—will come face-to-face with an animal filling up all of the available space in the passage, with little or no neck to get hold of, and wielding a large pair of well-sharpened incisors.

The subterranean tunnel systems of some burrowing animals are nearly as confusing as the catacombs, with passages overlapping, connecting, and abruptly dropping from and rising to the surface. A burrower expands its tunnel system as it grows in size and strength and refines its digging skills. Many rodents are such prolific tunnelers that almost all of their time is given over to digging in the earth, either expanding present burrows or abandoning them and starting new burrows elsewhere. Burrow tunnels are always just wide enough for the burrower itself to turn around in. A wider tunnel would require more energy than is necessary, but more important than this, the animal can act as a living plug and block off the passage to protect its young from an intruder or to present its teeth without exposing the rest of its body.

Most burrowers also dig several concealed entrances and exits to their burrows. They use these handy "plunge holes" for gathering food from distant places or to escape predators when they are caught up on the surface. They also use them as emergency exits from the burrow in the event of flooding or intrusion. The mazelike tunnel system of the woodchuck, which sometimes has passages connecting it to a completely separate and equally complicated burrow system, is all it needs to keep itself and its young safe from predators while under the ground.

All burrowers clear out at least two and often five or more chambers for sleeping, resting, breeding, rearing the young, storing waste, or hoarding food. Because rodents make up the primary food source of so many carnivores, all of whom possess a keen sense of smell, it would be impossible to keep the young safe from predation up on the surface. In the presence of large and powerful meat eaters such as wolves, coyotes, lynx and bobcats, bears, foxes, and the entire weasel family (whose long, slender bodies are designed for invading rodent burrows), the only safe place for a litter of helpless rodents is well beneath the earth.

TWO

A Prairie Dog's Town

T HE HOME RANGE OF THE PRAIRIE DOG, *CYNOMYS LUDOVI-cianus*, is the large, open prairies and plains of the West. Prairie dogs are less than one-third the size of a woodchuck or marmot, yet their underground burrow systems may extend for hundreds of acres. Before ranchers and farmers reclaimed most of its territories, the prairie dog was once a builder of vast underground "towns" that could cover thousands of square miles and house millions of prairie dog occupants. In the not too distant past, prairie dogs thrived alongside bison, which grazed long-grass prairies down to the shorter grasses preferred by both animals. Together they coexisted for centuries, the prairie dog towns expanding in size as the herds of bison moved across the plains.

The abundant grassy forage and deep, rock-free soil of prairies and plains are especially suited to the communal lifestyle of these small 3-pound tunnelers. When prairie dogs establish an area suitable for a colony, their burrows soon expand into a village, and the village—if left unmolested—soon grows into a large "town" composed of female-controlled coteries. Each coterie, or clan, consists of a male, three or four females, and a large group of youngsters. These subgroups of related prairie dog families all cooperate to monitor activities on their own turf and in the town at large, keeping a constant lookout for the local predators. Yet each coterie draws and protects its own

15

A typical prairie dog town is composed of a collection of female-dominated "coteries." Each small group includes a male and several females and youngsters. While prairie dogs are highly social animals and cooperate with the neighboring coteries within the town, all keep to their own clans, greeting and "frisking" each member as it leaves or enters the burrow to determine whether it belongs to the immediate family.

strict boundaries within the town and does not tolerate trespassing prairie dogs. To identify their clan mates, coterie members greet each other with a brief hug or nose-touching upon leaving and entering the burrow.

A prairie dog colony's circular, crater-shaped burrow entrance rests nearly rim-to-rim with its neighbors' craters like the checkers on a crowded game board. As with the groundhog's earth mound, the volcano-shaped crater surrounding the entrance hole to the prairie dog's burrow serves as an efficient lookout. But it also serves another, equally important purpose. Western prairies and plains can be almost instantly submerged under inches of rain after a heavy cloudburst. The flat prairies and plains often cannot absorb rainwater quickly enough to keep it from accumulating on the surface, and it pours into holes and crevices instead of soaking into the earth.

If it were not for the prairie dog's crater-shaped burrow entrance, which acts as a dike to hold the water back, the animal might soon be flooded out of its burrow. A particularly heavy rainstorm can even destroy the 2-foot-high crater, so it has to be constantly "coned up." The prairie dog shapes the crater up with its forepaws, tamping the loose soil down with its nose. Some may even insert thick grass stems into the surface of the crater to help keep it from eroding. Prairie dogs often survive prolonged storms or heavy flooding by holing up in an elevated burrow chamber containing a pocket of air. After a soaking rain, a colony of prairie dogs might be seen sitting on top of their partially submerged craters like so many mildly stunned homeowners wondering where the ground went.

A hole at the center of the entrance crater drops straight down for more than a dozen feet, abruptly turning sideways, then running horizontally with the surface for another 30 or so feet. The prairie dog digs side tunnels terminating in sleeping and defecation chambers and might add several quick-exit holes. Just below the opening to the burrow's crater-shaped entrance, the prairie dog excavates a small, shallow shelf off to one side of the tunnel. When the bark of a neighbor warns of possible encroachment on the town at large (with unblocked expanses of sky and land in full view, warning yips and barks

Western prairies and plains can be instantly submerged after a heavy cloudburst. When this happens, prairie dogs take to the tops of their raised burrow craters, which act as small dikes to hold back the water.

The prairie dog's burrow plunges straight down before branching off into side tunnels leading to sleeping, breeding, and waste chambers. A small side shelf near the burrow entrance allows the animal to stay hidden but within earshot of the upside world.

are issued routinely), the prairie dog dives headfirst into its burrow, spreading all four legs out against the sides of the tunnel to break its fall and to avoid dropping in a senseless heap at the bottom of the shaft.

A few moments later, the sound of an "all's well" call signals the end of the safety drill, and the tops of heads begin to emerge from the centers of a couple of craters, then a few more.

Finally an entire colony of partially visible prairie dog heads can be seen cautiously peering about. Curious by nature, prairie dogs cannot resist taking a peek to find out what has happened in their absence, even though moments earlier one of their own may have been carried off by a coyote or an eagle. Unless it is personally being pursued, after diving into its burrow a prairie dog usually retreats no farther than the small shelf just below the mouth of the entrance. Here it crouches and listens until a decent interval has passed before carefully raising the top of its head above the ground to see what is amiss.

Prairie dogs are standard fare for many animals, including coyotes, golden eagles, rattlesnakes, and burrowing owls. The snakes and owls often live full-time on the prairie dog preserve, taking over burrows near the edge of town from which they've evicted or eaten the owners. Here they raise their own young. The rare, nearly extinct black-footed ferret is a longtime foe of prairie dogs. A member of the weasel family with a body designed for chasing rodents through their own tunnels, the ferret evolved side by side with its primary source of food. Prairie dog extermination campaigns wiped out large numbers of both animals, in the end doing far greater damage to the black-footed ferret population.

The prairie dog's greatest enemy, however, may be the badger. This animal can send dogs flying from their burrows before it even begins to shovel them out with its powerful claws and forelimbs. Prairie dogs are safe from most predators while inside their burrows, but a badger is capable of boring through the prairie dog's burrow faster than the dog can crawl through its tunnels in search of an exit to the surface.

THREE

Pocket-Size Tunnelers

A SMALL RODENT OF NORTHERN PRAIRIES AND WESTERN meadows, the pocket gopher *(Thomomys talpoides)* has fur-lined cheek pouches, which it uses to store and transport not nuts and seeds as chipmunks and other rodents do, but soil. Its cheek pouches, or "pockets," can even be turned inside out for cleaning. The pocket gopher is able to seal off its ears and eyes to keep out dirt while working underground. It can tolerate low-oxygen conditions and has special hairs located throughout its fur that help orient it in darkness while it is engaged in its lifelong pursuit—tunneling in the earth.

The pocket gopher spends much of its life underground, mainly because much of what other animals must do above the ground it can do below. Its tunnels are designed for transportation and feeding as well as for sleeping, refuge, and breeding. In the heat of the night during the summer it comes to the surface to chew down plants—all too often garden plants—and drag them into its burrow, where it can eat in peace. Like all rodents, it has extremely strong, sharp teeth. The long digging claws of its forepaws resemble the curved tines of a garden fork. Both teeth and claws grow rapidly and nonstop throughout the animal's life, so the pocket gopher must whet them constantly by chewing and digging to keep them worn down. By the end of summer the pocket gopher will have amassed a large store of roots for the winter, although it continues to dig its tunnels all winter long.

The pocket gopher neatly carries excavated soil from its burrow in special fur-lined cheek pouches that can be turned inside out for cleaning.

The surest signs of the presence of a pocket gopher are the small, fan-shaped mounds of soil it excavates from its burrows. A single animal can tunnel hundreds of feet in a few months, making the gopher (more particularly, its mounds) a serious nuisance to farmers' expensive field machinery. But although they may be costly in one respect, pocket gophers know how to aerate the soil. A colony of them can move nearly half a dozen tons of earth per acre in one year. Their tunneling efforts are especially obvious after the snow melts. The surface of the ground is often scored with raised gopher tunnels radiating in all directions.

Gophers make two sets of tunnels. They dig one shallow network of interconnecting tunnels, with several feeding shafts to the surface, that runs just below the ground. They use these subsurface "roadways" for traveling safely and quickly from one place to another. The shallow system of tunnels also allows them to pop quickly above and below the surface in order to forage for food and to more conveniently harvest plant roots and tubers reaching just below the ground. Once a tunnel has been depleted of its overhanging garden of produce, the gopher seals it off for the season. This way it does not waste time and effort foraging in depleted food larders.

Pocket gophers dig a much deeper system of tunnels for nesting and breeding, for escaping from harm, and for shelter from the cold of winter and heat of summer. The gopher builds its nesting chamber deep in the ground, far below the frost line, where it is usually much warmer. (It cannot tolerate severe heat

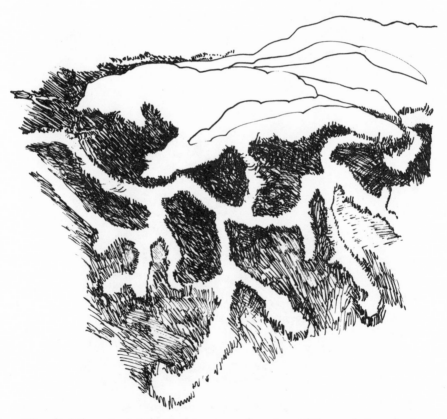

The slightly raised, labyrinthine tunnel system of the pocket gopher's burrow is easy to see just after snowmelt.

and will die very quickly in temperatures greater than 100°F.) When inside its burrow, the gopher always seals off its living quarters with a plug of soil to help keep out water as well as predators.

The male pocket gopher literally digs around for a mate, digging a straight-line burrow of more than 100 yards, if necessary, until it eventually runs into the burrow of a female gopher. Pocket gophers are extremely territorial, even toward their mates. Once the two gophers have mated, each partner seals its burrow off from the other's so there is no further contact. Unlike many other rodents, gophers produce small litters that average only about three young. The gopher's chances of making it beyond infancy are very good because so much of the animal's existence is carried out underground. The young are born completely helpless, yet by the time they are two months old they leave the parental burrow and begin digging their own feeding tunnels and living chambers.

The pocket gopher has special hairs located throughout its fur that help to orient it while it speeds along the dark tunnels of its miniature underground transportation system.

FOUR

The Most
Ferocious Digger

THE SCOURGE OF RODENTS EVERYWHERE WITHIN ITS range—which includes most of the central and western parts of the country—the badger might be said to be dabbling when it preys on pocket gophers and prairie dogs, for it can and does tackle much larger and fiercer prey. It has been known to kill and eat rattlesnakes it happens to run across while invading the burrows of its main diet, prairie dogs, and it can easily fend off attacks by animals much larger than itself.

A member of the weasel family, the American badger, *Taxidea taxus*, must represent something suspiciously close to a cosmic joke on rodents, which have evolved their unique burrowing behavior largely as a means of protection against a large and varied cast of predators just like this one. As the game goes, the rodent ensures its safety by digging tirelessly and staying alert. But the badger seems to break all the rules. It gets its reward not because it is fast or patient or slim enough, like the weasel, to wiggle into the tunnel after its prey, but because it has the sheer strength to wreck the rodent's home.

The badger has been called a bulldozer, a steam shovel, and a fighting machine (badgers used to be trapped and used in fights against dogs, contests that the badgers usually won). It

The badger's wide, heavily muscled body and long, powerful claws allow it to plow through the narrow tunnels of its primary prey, small rodents such as prairie dogs and pocket gophers. It can dig so swiftly that the rodents often cannot outrun it while trying to escape from their own burrows.

has a wide, low-slung profile and a bearlike face with a distinctive slash of white running over the top of its head and down between its eyes. The badger's coarse, grizzled fur resembles the fur of the grizzly bear, its primary predator. Long claws and sharp canines equip the badger with fearsome tools and weapons, and its heavily muscled, large-boned body gives it staying power while digging and fighting. Young badgers are vulnerable to coyotes and golden eagles, but a fully grown badger's only natural enemy is the grizzly. When the badger is threatened, it either escapes into its own fortresslike den or, if caught off guard, burrows into the earth on the spot, disappearing from view within moments.

The opening to the badger's burrow resembles the shape of its body: flat and wide. Badgers excavate huge burrows in proportion to their size, digging the tunnels up to 10 feet wide and 30 feet deep. The badger digs its den as though it were being hotly pursued, boring into the soil like a living earth auger. Dirt, rocks, and debris are scooped out with the front paws, tossed straight back under the stomach, and kicked out of the way with the rear feet in one continuous motion. When a badger is excavating at top speed, a solid spray of dirt fans out in the air behind it.

The badger wears its flesh and fur like a bulky winter coat. The loose hide makes it tough for another animal to get a solid grip on the badger, but this isn't the only purpose for it. When digging tunnels, a badger can abruptly swivel around within its own skin, digging upside down and twice as fast as it could if it were forced to stop and back out of the hole or had to labor to turn on its back when working on a narrow passage. It sleeps in a scooped-out chamber at the end of the tunnel. The badger

When threatened by a larger animal such as a bear, a badger can move the earth like a steam shovel and disappear from sight within a few moments.

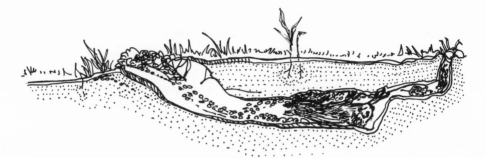

A badger can dig belly-up as easily as it can belly-down. This large weasel is able to revolve its body within its own skin as it burrows, allowing it to swiftly work all sides of a tunnel simultaneously. The badger's loose hide also makes it hard for larger predators to get a good, solid grip.

also digs a couple of escape hatches leading from its burrow, but there is rarely any need for this precaution.

Only the most confident animal would risk following the badger into the depths of its burrow. When confronted outside the den by something more threatening than itself, the badger dashes for the entrance to its burrow—keeping its head and teeth in full view of the enemy. Agile for all of its awkward-looking bulkiness, the badger can move backward as easily and quickly as it can run forward—which, admittedly, is not much faster than a brisk waddle.

Naturally, all of this digging gives the badger a constant appetite. In fact, any given area can support only a few badgers at a time, because more of them would soon clean out the local food supply. The badger uses its superb earth-moving skills to rout out ground squirrels, wreaking havoc on their burrows as it bores through their narrow tunnels faster than they can run. The badger is wily, too. It often digs connecting tunnels into a rodent burrow and lies in wait or plugs off its preys' escape holes before going in after them. A nocturnal hunter, the badger almost always feeds at night while ground squirrels are slumbering in their chambers.

The badger's less-than-subtle feeding activity often draws to the site coyotes, hawks, and other opportunists who know that easy-to-catch prey will soon be run out into the open. Of course, many prairie dogs, gophers, and other prey escape injury by holing up quietly in an overlooked chamber as the badger thrashes about in their burrow. Once the badger has eaten the burrow's occupants, it frequently sleeps off dinner in the newly enlarged den. Badgers also temporarily desert their own dens from time to time. But they seem to have a good grasp of the behavior of other animals, because they routinely go back to these old dens and prey on the rabbits and other animals foolish enough to seek shelter there.

FIVE

The Lair of the Trapdoor Spider

I T IS HARD TO RESIST COMPARING THE TRAPDOOR SPIDER TO an eccentric, unsociable recluse set in its ways. Somewhat fittingly, the trapdoor spider is found mostly in the southern parts of the country, from moist streambanks in Florida to dry and grassy areas of Texas, Arizona, and southern California. It spends nearly its entire existence alone inside its silklined burrow. Active at night, the trapdoor spider barely moves

beyond its burrow entrance to snag unwary prey before dashing back to the safety of its underground chamber.

A member of the Ctenizidae family, a group of soil-burrowing arachnids, the trapdoor spider is a squat, short-legged creature that has rows of tough digging spines on its front legs. The spider builds its burrow by shaping loosened soil into balls and moving them out of the way until the burrow is about 5 to 8 inches deep.

Because the trapdoor spider rarely leaves its burrow, it is extremely detail oriented in its construction techniques. It carefully waterproofs the walls of the burrow with a mixture of saliva and earth until they are smooth and hard, then lines the entire tunnel in layers of fine silk. The spider builds the burrow just wide enough to turn around in, and no wider. As the spider grows, it widens and deepens its tunnel and fastidiously layers it with more silk.

The most remarkable part of this structure gives the spider its name. The "trapdoor" operates exactly as the name implies. Although some burrow doors are made of thin silk designed to do little more than keep out the elements, the well-crafted "cork" door is a tiny marvel of joinery and function. It is a thick disk composed of compressed soil, saliva, and silk and attached to the burrow entrance by a carefully woven silken hinge. The spider builds the door starting with the hinge, which is especially critical to the door's operation. The edge of the door is carefully beveled by the spider to fit snugly into the burrow entrance, and the outside of the door rests flush with the ground.

The spider disguises the surface of its trapdoor with moss, dirt, and other debris so it blends in with the surroundings. When closed tightly, the door is almost impossible to detect. At night, the spider sits at the entrance of its burrow with the door slightly ajar. When opportunity knocks, so to speak, the spider pounces on its prey and drags it inside the burrow. The door swings shut by itself. The cork trapdoor is so well constructed that most would-be intruders cannot pry it open. The spider easily resists an outside pull on the door by holding it closed

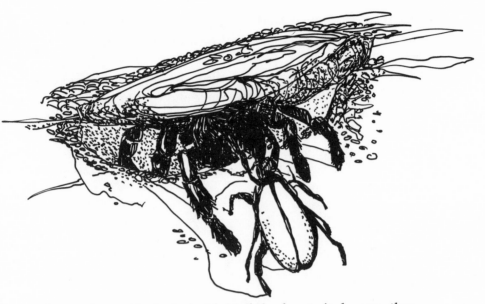

The trapdoor spider lurks just behind the door to its burrow, then leaps upon unwary insects. After the spider draws its prey back into its burrow, the "trapdoor" swings shut firmly on its own, sealing and camouflaging the spider's underground lair.

with its claws while it braces its legs against the burrow walls. In fact, it is even hard to pry the door open with a knife blade. Trapdoors that are manually forced open will later be closed by the spider after the coast has cleared.

Some trapdoor spiders build burrows with an extra chamber adjacent to the main burrow. This side chamber is sealed by yet another door. If the spider is followed into the burrow by an intruder it cannot fend off, it retreats into its side chamber and closes it off, leaving the puzzled gate-crasher in an apparently empty spider burrow.

This auxiliary chamber is particularly useful against the spider's worst enemy, the spider wasp. The spider wasp has an uncanny ability to locate trapdoors no matter how well they are concealed. Instead of prying the door open, the wasp chews through it, and once the wasp is inside the burrow, unless the spider can escape, the end is rather grisly. The wasp quickly stings it to death and lays its eggs on the spider's stomach. When the wasp larvae emerge, they awaken to their very first meal.

Like any well-insulated structure, the silk-lined burrow of the trapdoor spider is warm in winter and cool in summer and makes for a very secure nursery when the time comes. After mating, the spider eggs are hung up in sacs on the wall. When the young trapdoor spiders emerge, they continue to live in the burrow for many weeks before leaving to build their own small subterranean hideaways.

The Aerial Burrow of the Purse Web Spider

A CENTURY AGO SOME WOMEN CARRIED LONG, NARROW handbags made of finely woven metal mesh or beaded fabric. The female *Atypus*, or purse web spider, of the southeastern United States builds a home cum snare that is similar in appearance to these delicate nineteenth-century purses. The purse web spider's tubelike "aerial webs" are found running up the trunks of sweet gum, oak, and magnolia trees in Florida.

To construct her nest, the purse web spider digs a deep underground burrow into the earth. She lines the burrow in a dense layer of silk much like the trapdoor spider does. But the purse web spider does not seal her burrow off with a door. Instead, as she emerges above the ground she extends the tubular shape of the tunnel from the mouth of the opening by weaving a silk aerial burrow that runs across the ground or up the side of a tree trunk.

She excavates her tunnel in much the same way that the trapdoor spider does: by rolling soil into compact balls. But instead of tossing these balls aside, she painstakingly sifts the dirt and debris through the tight weave of the above-ground web, thus gradually camouflaging the web's outside surface with dirt and debris.

The purse web spider weaves an aerial "burrow" up the side of a tree trunk. The pendulous shape of the web resembles the meshlike purses used by women a century ago.

She works below and above the ground by turns, digging out the burrow as she weaves and camouflages the aerial web inch by inch. As she works on each section of the purse web, she carefully fastens it to the tree bark or ground.

The finished aerial purse web tube is 10 or so inches long and about 1 inch wide. The completed burrow is fully lined in silk and is much deeper than the aerial web is long. This arrangement easily offsets the lack of a door at the mouth of the underground burrow. In order to give chase to the spider, a

The dual-level burrow of the purse web spider extends from the base of the tree trunk down into the earth, where the excavated tunnel is lined with silk.

predator must first cut through the "fabric" of dirt, debris, and silk of the aerial web. This gives the spider plenty of time to flee deep into the recesses of her underground burrow before her pursuer gives up in frustration.

The spider hunts by waiting deep inside her burrow for signs of prey. When an insect moves over the purse web, sending vibrations into the burrow, she quietly crawls through the underground tunnel and up into the aerial web. She does not leave the web. Instead, she positions herself next to the prey and quickly stabs her fangs into the insect through the wall of the web. She then cuts through the tube, pulls the insect inside the purse web, and mends and recamouflages the rent in the silk wall. When she is finished eating, she discards all food remains through a small opening at the top of the purse web.

When it is time to mate, the male taps on the purse web to alert the female to his presence. If invited in, he then makes a tear in the wall of the web (which the female later repairs), works his way down the tube, and enters the burrow. After mating, the male retires from the outer world and remains in the burrow until he dies. When the young leave the nest, they move only a short distance away from the maternal home, and the females build their own miniature purse webs and burrows.

SEVEN

The Woodchuck's Home with a View

WOODCHUCK, GROUNDHOG, MARMOT—ALL ARE THE SAME basic animal. The woodchuck (*Marmota monax*) is a marmot that lives in the East. A slightly smaller cousin, the yellow-bellied marmot (from the French nickname for the animal, *marmotte*) lives in the West. Woodchucks and marmots are the largest members of the family of squirrels, which in turn are members of the largest order of all mammals, the rodents. Rodents share a common distinguishing trait that governs much of their behavior: They have extraordinarily strong upper and lower incisors. They are all gnawing animals, and the burrowing ground squirrels such as the marmots are perpetual diggers as well.

Because of its large numbers and wide geographic distribution, the woodchuck is by far the best known of the marmots. A highly adaptable animal, it inhabits wooded and open areas of the eastern and central United States as well as nearly all of Canada. What sets the woodchuck apart from the other marmots, which are far more sociable and mutually dependent, is its independent nature. In fact, the meaning of the woodchuck's species name, *monax*, is "solitary." But like all marmots, it is a living and breathing earthmover.

The woodchuck could not live in the wild without its burrow. So important is its underground system of tunnels and chambers to the animal's peace of mind and sheer survival that it constructs two permanent homes: a deeper, simply designed burrow for winter hibernation and a shallower, more complicated burrow for the active and perilous days of summer. In warm weather, most of the woodchuck's time is spent grazing and tunneling. Not content with a large summer burrow, it also excavates a number of temporary burrows not too distant from the main den. The woodchuck moves at a slow waddle at best, and it needs its emergency retreats whenever it is caught off guard up on the surface of the ground and a little too far from its main burrow.

A woodchuck has many predators and must constantly seek the safety of the earth. When caught unawares while foraging out on the surface, the woodchuck quickly drops into one of many handy "plunge holes" dug throughout its burrow system.

For the main entrance to its summertime burrow, the wood-chuck stakes out the sunny side of a hill with loose, well-drained soil. Here it will lie or sit on top of a large mound of excavated soil that it heaps in front of the entrance hole, survey-ing its territory for signs of life—including trespassing wood-chucks. When all is safe outside, it also will use the entrance mound as a place to bask in the morning sun. The woodchuck's ears, eyes, and nose are all located near the top of its head, allowing it to detect much about what is going on in the outside world without sticking its entire head beyond the burrow entrance.

The woodchuck digs rapidly and easily with its sharp claws and stout front legs, shoving rocks and soil out of the way as it works, but it would not be able to tunnel very far or very quickly without its powerful incisors. It needs these sharp teeth to cut through the tough, entangled roots found in the subsoil of pastures and meadows. Like all rodents, its teeth never stop growing, so it must use them constantly to wear them down. A life of grazing and burrowing is suited to just this purpose.

To begin the burrow, the woodchuck first excavates a narrow passageway, or "gallery," leading from the main hole. This tun-nel slants downward, going as deep as 6 feet in loose, sandy soil or 4 feet or less in hard and rocky soil. The texture of the soil and overall weather conditions (as well as the size and strength of the woodchuck) determine the depth, location, and slant of each tunnel. A large "turnaround" chamber is cleared out at the end of this first deep shaft running from the main entrance. This is where the woodchuck will go throughout the day to rest and eat or to retreat in a hurry.

Somewhere along the main passageway, the woodchuck takes off in another direction and excavates a long, narrow tun-nel that winds upward and then downward. This tunnel may extend anywhere from 10 to nearly 50 feet, depending upon the movability of the soil and the industriousness of the wood-chuck. The sinuous path of the tunnel will help protect it against flooding. At the end of this second passageway, the woodchuck clears out a circular nesting and sleeping chamber, a shallow area that it pads with dry grass and leaves. Here it sleeps warm and dry and protected against intruders.

The woodchuck has quite a few predators: Foxes, coyotes, bobcats, and dogs can easily take a slow-moving woodchuck above ground. Unlike other marmots, which actively warn each other about any sign of danger, it is every woodchuck for itself. Handy escape holes are imperative for all woodchucks at all times while feeding on the surface. Ideally, the escape hatch will be one of its own making. Many a fleeing woodchuck has dived into the wrong burrow only to be driven out by the rightful owner. Forced to make a beeline for the next available "plunge hole," the woodchuck either drops into the safety of its own burrow or is ejected once again.

Because the woodchuck must be adept at disappearing, it burrows incessantly, digging out any number of these plunge holes within its feeding range. The holes may drop directly into the underground corridors of its main burrow or into temporary burrows it excavates throughout its range for just these turns of event. A woodchuck is rarely caught off guard. If it is surprised while foraging, it simply drops into a nearby plunge hole (which is often disguised with foliage and other vegetation) and is home free in a moment. A plunge hole is dug just large enough to admit a woodchuck and nothing larger.

Though the woodchuck is vulnerable on the surface, it is a different matter below ground. If a predator such as a fox, which is actually somewhat smaller and lighter, manages to squeeze in after the woodchuck, it would be hard pressed to chase down its prey within one of the woodchuck's own familiar tunnels, any one of which may abruptly resurface or continue on, perhaps connecting with another large burrow and yet another network of twisting and winding tunnels. The woodchuck can easily lose a pursuer by scuttling along its own dark and confusing maze of tunnels or, when all else fails, by turning to face the enemy head-on with its sharp teeth.

An older and stronger woodchuck may excavate up to three or more burrows connected by a series of narrow and well-worn foraging paths on the surface. An acre of land may even hold half a dozen woodchuck burrows, including the permanent winter and summer burrows and several temporary shelters. Altogether, about 600 pounds of soil are excavated from an average burrow, which may consist of up to 50 feet of tunnels. The woodchuck cleans out its burrows regularly, shoving dirt and debris out of tunnel openings with its chest and forepaws and adding fresh soil to the main entrance mound.

Winter dens are much simpler in design and function. The woodchuck digs a deep, single-shaft burrow in the woods, often below the protective roots of a large tree or beneath a stone wall. From fall until spring, sustained by a layer of fat stored up from a summer's diet of clover, grass, corn, flowers, and fruit, it sleeps there in its hibernation chamber, safe from all intruders behind a small wall of soil with which it has blocked off the only entrance to its winter burrow. In most areas of the country, the woodchuck even sleeps right past Groundhog Day.

Known by westerners as the "rockchuck," the yellow-bellied marmot *(Marmota flaviventris)* is much more of a team worker than the woodchuck is. Communal by nature, adult marmots share their burrows with their own offspring and other adults. All participate in an elaborate surveillance system designed to keep the colony safe, especially in areas that have little protective covering.

Unlike woodchucks, rockchucks dig their burrows beneath huge boulders and the rubble of rockslides at the bases of mountains. But marmots also excavate many temporary burrows and "drop shutes" around their range, for their primary predators are apt to be more fierce than the woodchuck's. Marmots must be vigilant against the grizzly bear, which can lift aside large rocks with ease and dig them out of their burrows, and the carnivorous badger, a digger and burrower *par excellence*. They are also sought after by wolves and mountain lions, and young marmots are particularly vulnerable to eagles.

As a result, all yellow-bellied marmots take part in an elaborate warning system designed to help defend against predators. Standing high on top of a boulder, one marmot can survey the

Woodchucks are solitary animals and must see to their own safety without relying upon warning calls from other 'chucks. Still, they are very curious and stay constantly alert to the goings-on in their home range.

group's entire territory while the rest eat, work, and play above ground. The marmot has quite a repertoire of warning sounds, each communicating a different kind of outside intrusion, and one shrill, high-pitched whistle from a designated "sentinel" is more than enough to alert the whole colony to leap for cover. When at ease, marmots, like woodchucks, like to bask in the sun on large boulders or on top of the earth mounds they build at the entrances to their burrows.

EIGHT

The Bear's Seasonal Resting Place

B EARS ARE LARGE ANIMALS WITH APPETITES TO MATCH. Unlike other large animals, such as deer, few bears can survive the winter season by foraging for the scarce vegetation during the day and bedding down in the open at night. They instead must retreat into their dens when the food supply dwindles. Deep inside their earthen sleeping chambers, bears "feed" for four or five months off of a layer of fat built up during the warm season for just this purpose. When cold weather comes, most bears have to den up and slumber—they don't enter the deep biological slowdown of true hibernation—until their food reappears once again.

Bears develop a remarkably thick layer of fat, far more blubber than they will ever need to get through the inactive denning period. Calorie for calorie, this layer of fat contains more energy and nutrients than the bear could possibly harvest if it were to forage all winter long. Bears build up such a thick layer of blubber—sometimes as much as 4 or 5 inches—that in the past the fat was valued as much for cooking as the bear's flesh was for meat and its hide for fur.

Black bears are the smallest and most adaptable of the North American Ursidae. Because of its smaller size and wider

Despite their rotundity, bears are surprisingly nimble creatures. They can sprint across a broad, open space in an instant—especially if new-born cubs are nearby. The black bear, in particular, is an excellent tree climber. A thousand stinging honeybees are no match for this bear's taste for honey.

tastes in food, the black bear thrives in most habitats and in almost every part of the United States and Canada. The black bear, or *Ursus americanus*, weighs up to "only" about 600 pounds and eats everything from apples (they crave this fruit so much they sometimes become inebriated from eating too many windfalls) to insects, rodents, and even carrion. Throughout spring, summer, and early fall, it eats constantly, grazing on twigs, berries, buds, leafy plants, nuts, roots and tubers, insects, eggs, honey, and the honey bees themselves if they get in the way.

The black bear is also much more flexible in its denning habits than the other bears. While grizzlies dig dens that are carefully designed to help them survive their harsh western winters, a black bear may dig a hibernation den or may decide to wait out the cold season in a cave or a large hollow tree. In the South, many black bears do not even den at all because plenty of their regular foods—or good substitutions—are available throughout the year.

The grizzly, *Ursus arctos*, usually chooses its den site with greater care because its survival demands are far greater. The grizzly's primary concern is not starvation, because it also layers on a large amount of fat, but rather the cold. Its large fat reserves allow it to slumber for months without eating—in fact, the grizzly often emerges in spring with fat to spare—but it can easily die in a poorly chosen or improperly excavated den, because there is little margin for error in temperatures that routinely plummet to well below zero. Take into account that grizzly cubs are born in the den at the peak of winter, and it becomes even more apparent that grizzlies must contend with an extremely limited and challenging set of circumstances.

Snow is the grizzly bear's first and most important consideration. Far from posing a danger, snow is what keeps the animal warm and its den inviolate. As the Eskimos well know, snow is a first-rate insulator. Like all effective cold-air barriers, it helps retain the den's interior heat by slowing down and halting the movement of air currents. Still air conserves the heat, while moving air dissipates it. However strong a grizzly may be, it cannot close off its den by filling the entrance with soil or blocking it with rocks, so the bear carefully sites the den entrance to catch a solid cover from the largest snowdrifts.

The grizzly invariably dens up just before the first heavy snowstorm of the season, settling down to sleep shortly before the entrance is blanketed by a dense pile of snow. Grizzlies seem to be able to time their safe withdrawal from the outside world down to the first day of hibernation. Some bears will linger at a newly dug den entrance, browsing on vegetation and napping off and on as they slowly wind down for the season. At the last moment, they crawl into the den just as the first snowfall covers their tracks and obscures the location of their resting place.

Grizzlies dig their dens near the tops of slopes. The slant of the hillside, the direction it faces, the way the wind will blow, and the type of soil all are taken into account. The earth above the den must be deep enough, and there must be enough soil-anchoring vegetative cover, to ensure that the den will not collapse during hibernation. (Grizzlies build a fresh den every year because the old one usually does collapse over time.) On the other hand, the slope must be shallow enough to hold the snow that drifts across the entrance to the den. If the snow slides off or melts away, the temperature in the exposed den will plummet immediately, and in all probability the bear will freeze to death unless it can find other shelter.

Grizzlies do their best to dig their dens where they will not be discovered, but a certain sign of a bear den in progress or one that has been abandoned is a wide swath of soil spread out just beyond the den entrance. Grizzlies pull tons of earth out of the hillside when making their dens, shedding the dirt and rocks in a wide "apron" behind them. A bear needs only a few days' time to excavate its den before retreating into it for the winter, so soil dug from an occupied den usually is not visible for very long before it disappears under the snow.

The mouth of the den is dug just large enough to accommodate the bear and nothing more. The entrance to the den tunnels deep into the hillside for half a dozen feet or so, slanting upward slightly. The upward slant of the tunnel helps keep the den dry, but its main purpose is to direct heat upward into the denning chamber. Both sexes build similar dens, but the small

In the mountains of the western United States and Canada, grizzlies and brown bears den high up on the sides of slopes. Great care is given to the selection of the den site: If it does not get blanketed by a deep, insulating snowdrift, the bear will freeze to death during hibernation.

size of the entrance is especially significant for a female bear with young to protect. Wolves as well as adult male grizzlies that emerge early from their own dens sometimes prey upon newborn grizzly cubs. If the female is fit and alert, would-be predators are apt to find not the cubs but mother grizzly herself filling the entrance to her den. They would be hard pressed to pass her to get at the cubs.

The hibernation chamber, like the den opening, is large enough only for the bear. When yearling bears go into hibernation with their mother for their first winter, extra space is made

A bear uses its long, raking claws to grub for insects, mark trees, snag rodents and fish, and tear out soil and rocks when building its den.

for them. Otherwise, a larger space would be less efficient. The smaller the sleeping chamber, the easier it is to keep it warm. Sometimes in spring, more bears emerge than denned up. Newborn grizzlies, like all bear cubs, weigh less than a pound at birth, so little extra denning space is needed for them. A female becomes pregnant well before entering the den, but a biological process known as "delayed implantation" allows the actual fertilization of the egg to take place much later, after the mother is well into hibernation. If the young were born earlier, she would have to suckle them all winter long, using much more energy and nutrients than necessary. Newborn grizzly cubs are born in January or February, not long before the new family leaves the den to forage for the new plant growth that is also just emerging.

When properly made, the hibernation chamber becomes a life-sustaining earthen womb. While they are active during spring and summer, grizzlies travel a home range that stretches for thousands of square miles. In the only home a grizzly will know for several long months out of the year, too much attention cannot be paid to providing warmth and comfort. The walls of the hibernation chamber are made as smooth as possible. Rocks are plucked out and tough roots are bitten away. A thick bedding of dead leaves, evergreen boughs, twigs, moss, and even some bear hairs are layered together to make a soft, cushioning bed several inches deep. The bedding's loose, fibrous material absorbs, retains, and returns the bear's own

Bear cubs—usually two—are born inside the den during the mother's hibernation. They emerge with her in the spring, spend their first summer with her, then return to the den to hibernate with her the following winter.

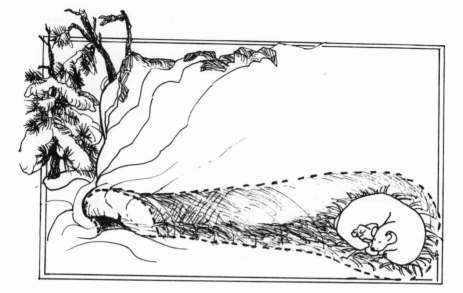

*Bears often excavate their winter dens directly beneath the roots of a
tree to help stabilize the soil above the entrance to the burrow.
The scooped-out hibernation chamber is densely cushioned with dead
leaves and other soft debris for the long slumber ahead.*

body heat, and together they help maintain the chamber's overall temperature, which stays considerably warmer than the outside air all winter long.

Older, more experienced grizzlies sometimes reach a surprising level of sophistication in their den construction. Some
bears take the slanting-tunnel concept a step further by
abruptly terminating the tunnel in a dogleg just before it opens
out into the sleeping chamber. At least one grizzly's den chamber was reached deep inside a hillside at the end of a long,
winding tunnel. Any extra bends and curves in the den's entrance tunnel further reduce the flow of cold air into and the
loss of warm air from the hibernation chamber. A grizzly will
often dig its den just below the thick spreading roots of a large
tree, which considerably strengthens the roof of the den and
helps to hide the den entrance as well.

Polar bears also den up for short periods of time, even though they have a more reliable food supply all year long, their main source of food being seals and other marine life. These huge, long-legged bears weigh up to twice as much as full-grown grizzlies. Polar bears sometimes retreat to summer dens, burrowing deep into the permafrost to escape the heat. Unlike grizzlies, which build fresh dens every year, generations of *Ursus maritimus* will use the same dens again and again. Some dens are used for hundreds of years.

Polar bears have to take into account avalanches as well as the deep cold when building their dens. Like grizzlies, they excavate their dens on the sheltered sides of ridges or slopes to take advantage of snowdrifts. The den entrance is sited as much as possible to capture the heat of the sun and to avoid the wind.

At the end of hibernation, a polar bear bursts through the wall of snow covering its hillside den. The quickest route to level ground is often a slide down the snowy slope.

Pregnant polar bears excavate their dens in October or No-
vember, burrowing 10 or so feet deep into the snow. The inside
temperature of the den's snow-walled chamber becomes considerably warmer than the outside air, and it stays that way.
Despite the polar bear's far greater weight, the entrance to its
den is roughly the same size or even smaller than the grizzly's.
The polar bear has no trouble squeezing into a tunnel of this
size because of its relatively narrow chest. Much of a polar
bear's weight is concealed by its long legs and long body.

The tunnel slopes upward to a sleeping chamber. This
chamber is a couple of feet higher and wider than the grizzly's
and is vented by a hole for discharging old air and letting in
fresh air. If the polar bear's hibernation chamber were sealed off
as the grizzly's is, the heat would soon cause the walls to melt
and turn to ice, which in turn would lower the temperature and
cut off most of the bear's air supply. The walls sometimes ice
over anyway, and when this happens, the drop in temperature
awakens the polar bear, which scrapes the ice off and checks
the ventilation hole. After the female gives birth, she widens
the chamber area so the cubs can move around and exercise as
much as possible before going outside. Once the bears break
through the barrier of snow over the den entrance, they have to
make their way straight down the steep, slippery slope.

PART TWO

Walls Without Windows

A BUILDING IS A SPACE ENCLOSED BY THE JOINING OF WALLS and a roof. But the shape an enclosed shelter takes on can vary tremendously, from the basic box of a typical house to the cone of a beaver's lodge, the flask-shaped vessels of the potter wasp and the swallow, and the assymetrical "multiple-unit" structures of honeybees and paper wasps.

Like our own homes, these load-bearing shells built by animals must be waterproof, snowproof, windproof, and intruderproof. They must be warm or cool in winter and summer, and they must be structurally sound enough to bear the weight of the inhabitants and their ceaseless activities. The building materials must be cheap and plentiful and light enough to transport and erect. The basic building plan and the home site must allow for renovation and expansion. And the home must be near a plentiful food supply and as far away as possible from troublesome neighbors.

Finally, and most important, the home must accommodate the various and changing needs of its inhabitants. The primary purpose of any animal's home is to provide shelter and safety for the young. Until they are old enough to leave the nest, young animals are vulnerable to predators. They lack the strength and skills to run for cover or to forage for food. The nursery, therefore, is the most important feature of any animal's dwelling.

Honeybees and paper wasps must produce large broods in order to have enough workers to collect food for the colony and to help with the construction of the hive. Fewer bees and wasps would mean less food and hive building, but a large colony produces a large hive, which translates to greater longevity and defense through strength in numbers. This is why many animals colonize. The thousands of cells found in these hives are designed to allow quick and solid construction for the burgeoning broods. No suitable building materials are available for the special construction needs of honeybees and wasps, however. The lightest building materials found in the natural world—insect silk and plant down—are too fibrous to mold into the delicate walls of the hive's cells to house the brood, let alone to hold the honeybee's large stores of pollen, nectar, and honey.

Therefore, wasps and honeybees have no alternative but to manufacture or process their own building supplies, which as it turns out are far superior for their purposes to anything else around. Wax and sticky paper pulp are easy to mold into the tissue-thin cell walls, and new wax and paper cells can be added quickly and easily as the colony explodes during the height of the summer season. All of the necessary building materials are at the nest site. The honeybee produces wax from its own body, and the paper wasp gathers wood pulp for its nest from the very wood to which the nest is attached.

The hives of both can withstand tremendous downward tension. The paper wasp's bulky hive hangs from a few strands of paper fibers, yet it carries the load of several thousand larvae as well as the weight of the adult wasps gathering at the nest to feed them. Honeybee combs can carry gallons of honey without spilling a drop or drowning the larvae in unconverted nectar. The broods of both have strict heat and humidity requirements, and bees and wasps have worked out ways to raise and lower the temperature in their hives at will. Wax and paper hives also can resist high winds and rain, and predator control is accounted for by the arrangement of entrances and the alertness of guards from the worker castes.

An anthill is as complex as a hive in attention to detail. Larvae are housed in special nurseries and shuttled from one place in the hill to another as their developmental needs change. Ants also take great pains to guard their nests, and although they are not as limited in their choice of building materials, they are extremely fussy about minute arrangements of the grass, twigs, and other matter they place on the tops of their hills.

The nests built by bees and ants are eerily similar to the ancient underground catacombs found near Rome and elsewhere in the world. In these subterranean tombs, small, sealed burial vaults were carved into the walls of mazelike passages that lead in places to large, open burial chambers. Likewise, live honeybee larvae are shrouded in spun silk and sealed within their individual waxen cells, which line a series of "beeways," or passages inside the hives. And many ants excavate special burial chambers within the underground portions of their nests, where they inter the bodies of their dead workers and drones.

At the other end of the home-building spectrum, beavers will put virtually anything into their dams and lodges, including boating accessories, tools and equipment, food containers, and other man-made items left near their building sites. Beavers are amazingly strong animals and are capable of cutting down and hauling saplings and large tree limbs over great distances back to their lodges and dams. The bulkiness of their lodges of wood, stones, and mud provides tremendous compression strength, enough so that the breeding chambers inside the upper portion of the lodge are safe from any possible collapse of the lodge walls.

Beaver kits raised in traditional "castle" lodges are protected from predators by the surrounding "moat" of deep water. When old enough to leave the nest, the kits are instructed by the adults in the skills of dam and lodge building. These small recruits embark immediately into the family building trade, learning how to cut and transport wood, weave mud and sticks together, and make the constant repairs that a large beaver compound requires, especially at the beginning of spring after winter snow and wind have taken a serious toll. The beaver's food and building materials are one and the same. It eats the bark and leaves from the very branches it harvests for its lodges and dams.

These particular animal buildings are rarely camouflaged. There is nothing quite so exposed as an anthill, yet the density of the earthen mound, the mazelike tunnel system of the inner reaches of the hill, and the sheer volume of ants are protection enough against most intruders. (Ironically, the honeybee's main enemies are not bears or people, but hordes of invading ants.) While birds and burrowing animals often take great pains to make their homes blend in with the landscape, hives, beaver lodges, and anthills are all remarkably obvious additions to the landscape.

More than anything else, it is the design and structural strength of these shelters that keep the inhabitants safe. Unlike most bird nests and underground burrows, such homes are meant for long-term use and are solidly built to last for many generations. All of the members of the colony become intimately acquainted with the neighborhood, so to speak, and fine-tune their behavior to the local environment. They learn how to coordinate building and breeding with the specific weather conditions of the area. They discover the whereabouts of favorite foods and the superiority of certain building materials over others. Except for the wasps, all of these animals cache food in their nests for wintering over. Bees put up pollen and honey, the ants store seeds and other plant foods in special chambers, and beavers cache a supply of food branches under the water near their lodges. When such care has been taken to build and stock a home, it is not easily abandoned. It is more likely to be expanded and renovated year after year, and in the process, some of these animals learn how to refine and improve their building skills to remarkable degrees.

NINE

The Honeybee's Waxen Retreat

H OW MIGHT YOU WORK OUT THE PROBLEM OF STORING SEV-
eral gallons of viscous liquid on a vertical plane inside
an irregularly shaped space? What if, additionally, some dry
substances must be kept separate from the liquid, and hundreds of unborn organisms must be housed within this same
space? Say you also have to allow for constant wear and tear
within the space by thousands of very active individuals com-
ing and going at all times, and to top things off, you have no
instruments for measuring or materials for building.

In order to solve this problem, you would have to be a
honeybee. *Apis mellifera* holds within its genes the blueprint to
nature's ultimate engineering feat—the honeycomb. Honey is
the very lifeblood of a wild honeybee colony, which has anywhere from thirty thousand to sixty thousand members to
nourish and protect. A hive of queen, workers, drones, and
unborn brood needs a supply of 400 to 500 *pounds* of honey to
survive for just one year.

It is the geometric principles embodied within each hexagonal cell of the honeybee's waxen home that make it possible to
hold all of a colony's honey, pollen, and brood without its pour-
ing to the ground in a sticky mass. The basic aim of honeycomb

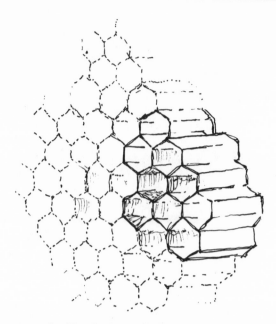

*The wax hexagonal cells of a honeybee's comb are engineered for rais-
ing the bee brood and storing honey and pollen. The cells point
outward and slightly upward, so uncapped honey does not flow out.
Because honeybees are able to regulate the temperature within the
nest, the tissue-thin walls of the cells retain their shape even in the
warmest weather.*

construction is to work with the least amount of material to
create the greatest amount of usable space. Honeycomb cells
must be strong enough to support many times their own
weight in honey. They also must be the right shape and size
to cradle the hive's constantly replenished brood. From egg to
larva to pupa, each honeybee gains one thousand times its own
weight before emerging, and it is physically active at different
times while in its cell. There is constant cleaning and repairing
going on in and around the hive at other times, and a great deal
of foot traffic adds to the general wear and tear as nectar and
pollen are delivered, processed, and stored by thousands of
worker bees around the clock.

The material-to-use ratio is important for another reason,
too. Honeybees must produce their comb-building material

from their own bodies, and it comes at a premium. Bees must collect several times the amount of nectar needed to make the honeycomb, or as much as 20 pounds of honey per pound of wax. It is estimated that at least twenty thousand nectar-gathering trips to the field are needed to produce just 1 pound of honey. Such a huge expenditure of energy makes beeswax an extremely expensive building material. Yet no other substance could possibly perform so well.

Honeybee colonies reproduce by swarming. Although wild honeybees will nest inside walls or hang their combs from tree limbs if the light is right (they need low light to produce wax), they most often nest inside hollows in live trees. When the time comes for half of the bees to split off from the parent colony to find a new home, the new hive must make haste. A fresh comb

The honeybee siphons nectar from flowers through tubelike mouthparts and gathers pollen on the hairs of its body. It combs the pollen from its body with its legs and packs it into a "pollen basket" on its hind leg. When the foraging bee returns to the nest, the hive workers will help it unload its cargo of pollen.

has to be built, a brood laid, and honey collected, processed, and stored in time for the following winter if the bees are to survive. Scouts are sent out to look for a suitable nest site while the new colony waits for them to report back. When different new home sites are found, the scouts return and convey to the colony through various "dances" the direction and distance of each nesting site. The sun's position is used to mark the location of a site, and the length of a dance tells the colony how far away it is. A few bees may leave and inspect the new locations themselves, then return and report their own impressions by dancing. Eventually a single site is decided upon. When all are in agreement, only one dance is performed. The colony then swarms around its queen and makes off en masse for its new home.

By this time, some of the scouts are already doing preliminary work on the new nest site by measuring out the cavity — pacing the surfaces of the interior to gauge the amount of area that will soon be filled with comb. The size of the cavity opening is particularly important, because the brood cells are usually located near here. It must be small enough to seal up in winter and easy to defend, if necessary. Guard bees will be stationed at the nest entrance to help warn of intruders such as ants and small rodents. Honey and pollen collected by the field bees will be stored near the top of the comb, farthest away from the main opening.

While some of the field workers forage for nectar, others collect a substance called *propolis* in great quantities. Harvested from the buds of trees and woody plants, this reddish brown sticky material is the honeybee's all-purpose varnish, sealer, glue, putty, and weatherproofer. Without it the nest would be vulnerable to parasites, water, and drafts. Honeybees seem to be repulsed by any foreign matter in or around their nesting site and will even coat small dead rodents with propolis when they cannot be carried out of the nest. Propolis is brought back to the nest on the legs of field bees, who deliver it to the hive workers. Propolis must be collected during the warmest part of the day, while it is still sticky and malleable. It dries to a hard, glossy sheen.

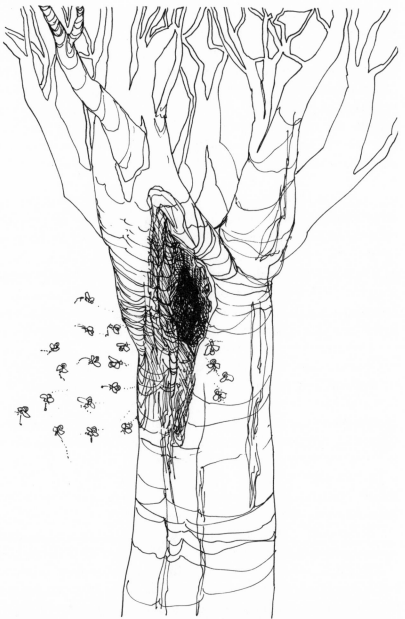

Honeybees "spring clean" a new nesting cavity by carrying out every bit of loose debris they can move. What they cannot move, including dead insects and small mammals, they seal over with a coating of propolis, a remarkable varnishlike resin gathered from wood and plant fibers.

Well before the first dab of wax is applied to start the combs, honeybees thoroughly "spring clean" their tree cavity, clearing out every speck of debris, including loose and rotted wood, twigs, leaves, and dead as well as living insects. Anything undesirable and unmovable is varnished with propolis. They then varnish every crack and crevice of the cavity until it is thoroughly sealed. Thousands of workers gather the propolis needed to varnish the tree cavity, as many thousands more glut themselves on the nectar they will need to produce wax for the comb.

The worker bee has four pairs of wax glands on her stomach. When it is time to produce the wax for the comb, honeybees hang in a still, dense cluster inside the hive until their temperatures rise and the wax begins to flow. Soon eight miniscule bars or flakes of whitish wax appear inside the bee's stomach pockets. These are scraped off by the legs, then chewed and kneaded with the mandibles until the wax is the right consistency for molding and building the cells of the honeycomb.

The precision and consistency of the cells in a wild honeycomb is amazing. Not only must all of the thousands of individual cells be uniform in size according to their function, but the half dozen or so combs hanging parallel to one another must be fitted into a space as irregular in shape as each tree cavity is different. From the time worker bees add their first daubs of wax to the top and sides of the cavity surfaces where the combs will be attached until they complete the comb, they must make minute adjustments to their work as they fill the tree cavity. Time is not wasted and mistakes are not made.

Honeycomb building codes are strict. Honeybees require "beeways," or bee corridors, of $1/4$ to $3/8$ inch wide between the combs, just the right width to admit the passage of one bee only. It is along these passageways that bees move within the hive, storing and treating the nectar and pollen and tending to the brood. Anything narrower is filled with propolis; anything larger is filled in with thicker transitional pieces of burr or brace comb. Whether the finished nest of combs is 5 feet or only 5 inches long, these beeways and the individual comb cells remain uniform in size. Propolis is the honeybee's equalizer. Al-

The gaps between sheets of honeycomb are called "beeways." These narrow corridors are used by the worker bees to move about the nest when filling the cells with honey and pollen. Each beeway is exactly the size of a honeybee, no more and no less.

though it is time-consuming to collect, it is not used sparingly. It shores up stress points throughout the comb, fills in irregular spaces, and strengthens the individual cells.

With thousands of honeybees working in concert, somehow coordinating their efforts without confusion, the wax is gradually expanded, molded, and shaped into vertical walls. The cells are "drawn" from each side of these walls to exacting specifications. The hexagonal shape of the cells is remarkably suited to the stress of honey and pollen storage and to brood raising. Considering that a piece of honeycomb weighing not much more than an ounce must hold about 4 pounds of honey, and that it takes several pounds of honey to make a pound of wax, a very strong, very stable, yet extremely lightweight design is an imperative, not a choice.

The hexagon is the only shape that will do. Aside from the fact that the hexagon is inherently stronger than other geometric forms, it also uses the least amount of material for the greatest amount of space. Each of the six walls of every hexagonal cell shares a wall with the cells surrounding it. There is no wasted wax. The walls of circular cells would barely meet and a large amount of unused space (and wax) would be wasted. Square cells, though weaker, would share walls with other cells as hexagons do, but then excess space would be wasted on the brood, which are relatively round. To further strengthen the comb as well as the individual cells, the honeybee draws out the cells so that the base of each cell rests upon the juncture of three cell walls on the opposite side. In other words, cell bottoms, unlike cell walls, are not shared.

Each honeybee adds its own wax, then gradually draws out and thins the cell walls. When it has built as much wall as it can, it leaves a thickened "coping" at the top of the wall. This thicker ledge will be strong enough to bear the weight of the next worker, which in turn adds wax and continues to draw the cell walls outward and upward. Each worker takes up precisely where the last left off, so that each cell within a given section of comb is finished to the blueprint's instructions: 1/5-inch-wide cells for worker brood, 1/4-inch-wide cells for drone brood and honey storage. All honeycomb cells are 5/8 inch deep and exactly twenty-five cells to the square inch. The wax is molded so finely that it would take up to three thousand cell walls to make an inch.

Before honey is stored or eggs are deposited in the cells, the interiors of the cells are polished and coated with propolis to keep them as dry and germ-free as possible. Brood and food cells are always capped. But instead of producing more precious wax to cap the cells, honeybees pull wax out of the thickened coping of the cell walls themselves to form the caps. The outside surfaces of the cell caps are always polished. The rough underside of the cap is used by the larva to orient itself so it knows which way to break out of the cell when it is time to emerge.

Even as the comb is being built, field bees are delivering nectar, which must be stored in the newly created cells. But before the honey can be capped, sealed, and stabilized, the water must be evaporated from the nectar. This is what helps convert it to honey. To evaporate the water, the honeybees beat their wings over the uncapped nectar until it reaches the right consistency. The nectar and uncapped honey do not pour out of the comb because the cells are canted upward slightly, taking advantage of gravity.

Like a complex, artificially regulated high-rise office building, the honeycomb has special temperature needs and the means to control it. Eggs and larvae require a constant 95° F temperature, yet their delicate wax "incubators" will begin to melt and run in even slightly hotter weather during the height of summer. Humidity must be kept at a very constant 40 to 50

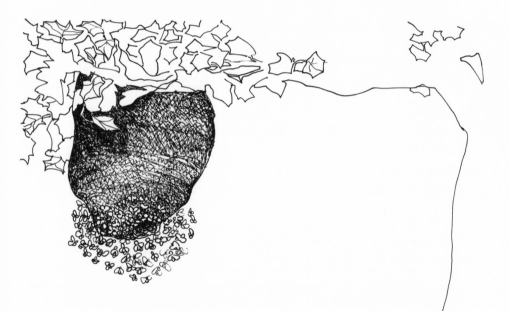

On a hot day, worker honeybees swarm around the entrance to the hive and fan the air with their wings until the inside temperature drops and the excess moisture evaporates. If the temperature is extremely high, other workers will carry cold droplets of water into the hive and place them on the individual cells to cool them down even faster.

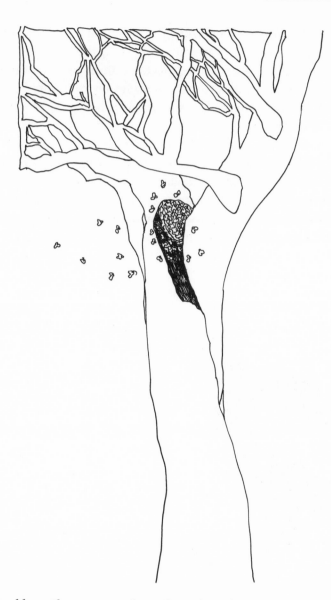

When cold weather comes, a honeybee colony forms a "winter cluster."
In the fall, the colony stops raising brood and eats honey and a great
deal of pollen, which is converted to protein and fat. The bees then
pack themselves about the hive, some crawling into empty cells. The
mass of bee bodies generates considerable heat, and as the honeybees
on the outside of the cluster become cold, those on the inside change
places with them.

percent, yet nectar processing swiftly increases the amount of moisture in the air.

When hive temperatures move out of the correct range, worker honeybees communicate the problem to the colony at large, and the bees halt all other work to station themselves at various hive openings. There, they furiously fan their wings, simultaneously drawing out warm air and pulling in cool air. During a serious heat wave, other worker bees may carry droplets of water into the hive and place them on the cells to cool them. So intently may a large hive of honeybees fan their nest on a hot summer's day, that the noise of hundreds of small wings beating the air may be heard far from the hive.

TEN

The Ant's Earthen City

I F YOU PLACE THE PALM OF YOUR HAND ON THE SURFACE OF an anthill at midday, your first response might be that something inside was cooking away. So startling is the amount of warmth that emanates from the surface of an exposed anthill that it does not seem possible that it could be generated by the sun alone. Yet from morning until early evening, the raised surface of an anthill will remain two to three times as hot as the ground immediately around it. Some ants even take advantage of this heat. Wood ants often sun themselves on top of their hills before going inside, where their bodies then act as small heat generators to warm an interior chamber.

An anthill mound absorbs so much heat not only because it is higher than the surrounding area, but also because it is drier and more fibrous. A large, long-established hill represents the work of many generations of ants, thousands upon thousands of tiny miners that continually hoist particles of soil much heavier than themselves to the surface.

A mature anthill is similar to a pomegranate or a nautilus shell in that its plain, rounded surface conceals a surprising complexity within a mostly hollowed-out core. An anthill's multiple storage, waste, and brood chambers are interconnected by an intricate series of ever-lengthening tunnels and galleries. Galleries are open passages or balconies that run

The raised mound of an anthill captures so much heat from the sun that it becomes several degrees hotter than the surrounding area. When they reach a certain age, ant larvae are brought from below-surface chambers of the anthill up to warmer chambers within the hill itself.

alongside chambers and interconnect with the tunnels. Smaller antechambers just inside the nest entrances feed into larger chambers that are specially excavated for food and nesting. Over time, the ceilings, walls, and floors of the chambers inside an anthill become extremely smooth and even from the constant daily movement of the worker ants as they travel around.

The subterranean portion of an anthill is connected to the hill by tunnels and galleries, which either drop straight down or are sloped to provide good water drainage. As an ant colony grows, the underground nest grows with it, extending downward and outward. The brood and queen ants are usually kept in the deepest, safest chambers within the nest. Along narrow, ant-size passageways, the workers constantly scurry, carrying food from the field down into storage chambers below or mov-

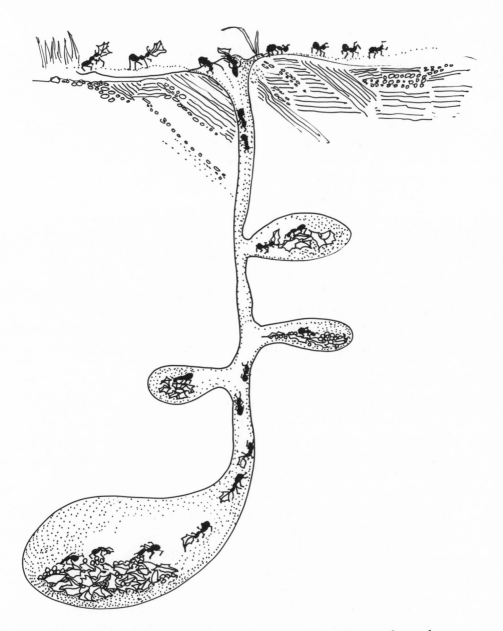

The underground portion of an anthill is easily as deep as the surface mound is high. Here in the earth, the ants excavate a complex system of tunnels and galleries leading to special chambers for breeding, food and waste storage, and even burying the dead.

ing older brood up into the warmer chambers within the hill itself to take advantage of the additional heat inside the hill.

Ants understand how to manipulate and take advantage of the widely varying temperatures inside their nests. Because brood pupae need extra warmth yet are resistant to dryness, when the time comes they are carted to warmer chambers inside the upper mound. On the other hand, eggs and young larvae can get by with much less heat but need considerably more moisture, so they are kept inside the "nursery chambers" deeper within the ground.

Given the vagaries of the seasons, an anthill is structurally quite sound. Coarse vegetation is used on the inside of a hill, while finer materials are laid on the outside surface to create the "nest mantle." The coarse materials give strength and stability to the structure, while the finer stuff, much like fiberglass insulation, helps guard against heat loss and resist the rain. Nest entrances are closed off at night to conserve heat and are opened up during the day to stimulate air circulation inside the nest.

Some ant colonies take advantage of the local vegetation to shore up their nests. Long, tough-stemmed grasses may be left to grow completely through the surface of an anthill mound, helping to camouflage it somewhat while keeping it exposed to the heat of the sun. The shallow roots of the grass help strengthen the dome mantle, and the bases of the grass stems are often used as ramps leading into the "doors" of the nest. The grass stems also help to obscure the entrances, which are not much larger than the stems of the grass itself.

The nest entrances in a grass-covered mound are often hidden like so many small, barely noticeable adobe doors around the base of the anthill where it meets the ground. And what appears to be random debris on the surface of an anthill turns out on closer inspection to be carefully arranged cut-up plant material. No one but the ants knows exactly what purpose these scattered bits and pieces of debris serve, but whenever this "debris" is added to or disturbed, the following day the ants' debris is usually found rearranged in its original position and the foreign matter removed from the hill.

Large harvester ants in the western United States build perfectly peaked gravel mounds, which they cover with reflective
lava particles or sand. Their mounds are often a foot or more
high. The interior chambers of these remarkable anthills are
carefully laid out to accommodate seed storage and brood raising. Harvester ants tend to prefer shiny, heat-reflecting materials for their hills—everything from broken glass to fossilized
shark teeth has been found covering the surface of these large,
pyramid-shaped mounds. In the spring, the ants work to clear
all of the brush and other vegetation for several feet from
around the perimeter of the mound. In order to do this, they

*Harvester ants gather seeds, berries, grass, bees, grasshoppers, bee-
tles, and other food for storage in their large, circular "granaries"
inside the hill. Some of the food is processed before storage. The harvester ant makes "ant bread" out of seeds by converting the starch
to sugar.*

must climb each plant and bit by bit tear up and chew every one down to the ground.

A large city of harvester ants may reach half a million in population. The labors of such a large colony of ants are endless: Queens lay their eggs, worker ants nurse the queens and their broods, others feed the grubs, collect and store food, make repairs to the hill, carry and bury the dead, and move the brood from chamber to chamber as they grow up. Berries, grass, seeds, bees, grasshoppers, beetles, and other edibles are transported through tubular tunnels and galleries and stored inside circular granaries or storerooms that are only an inch high and a few inches wide. Some of the food is processed before storage. Harvester ants make "ant bread" by chewing up seeds. The ants' saliva converts the starch to sugar; these "loaves" are then stored away in special "pantries."

Another talented food processor, the town ant (*Atta texana*) of the southern United States, is known for the "fungus gardens" it grows inside special chambers. These fungus-growing chambers may be nearly a foot across, and the subterranean portions of this large ant's colonies have been known to reach up to 5 acres in size. Leaf harvesting is the town ant's particular specialty. Foraging paths leading from the nests are beaten down with the comings and goings of long columns of ants. Thousands of ants are needed to collect the leaves necessary for growing the fungus, which serves as food for the entire colony throughout the year. Every day the large leafcutters go forth single file from the nest, each returning with a cut leaf several times its size and carried above its head like an oversize umbrella.

The leaves delivered by the harvesters are first composted and then treated by the queen. Heat and moisture must constantly be adjusted to stimulate and maintain the growth of the fungi, much like a commercial mushroom operation requires specific levels of darkness, heat, and humidity to produce the mushrooms. The ants must provide the precise conditions needed to grow the fungi. A specific number of passageways connected to the surface are constructed in order to draw in

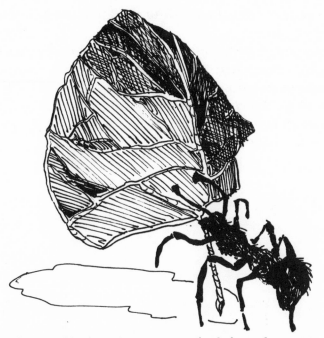

A special caste of leaf-cutting ants goes forth from the nest to gather the colony's food. The leaves are treated by the queen and composted in special "fungus gardens" inside the anthill.

oxygen and vent the gases produced by the growing fungi. By constantly opening up and closing off the fungus-garden chambers, the ants control the gas exchange and humidity level just as a gardener ventilates a greenhouse.

Older colonies of town ants often must dig long tunnels to connect the nest to distant forage sites when the immediate area has been defoliated. These distant tunnel exits are marked by small craters of excavated soil.

The individual ants vary greatly in size, depending upon their occupations within the colony. Smaller town ants are bred and recruited to tend the fungus gardens and to feed and nurture the young. Larger, stronger ants go out into the field to harvest the leaves, while the biggest of all act as sentries or soldiers to guard the entrances to the anthill and to ward off intruders.

At the end of the warm season, an ant colony vacates its hill and moves deeper into the ground for protection against the cold; without the strong summer sun, the anthill loses its heat. In the spring, the colony reemerges and immediately goes to work repairing whatever damage the winter wind and cold weather have done to the hill.

ELEVEN

The Hornet's Paper Abode

T HE BALD-FACED HORNET, ONE OF THE SO-CALLED "PAPER wasps," is the builder of the familiar turnip-shaped nest that we are forever admonished not to disturb. Actually, the nest may be perfectly round or shaped like a football or even an eggplant, and may reach nearly a foot and a half in length. Black with yellowish white markings, *Vespula maculata* is one of the few true social wasps and lives in colonies as large as twenty thousand. All but the queen die each year at the onset of winter, but the amazing paper nest that is so skillfully pasted together by the queen and her workers usually survives and is used again and again by many new generations of hornets. Although the Chinese are usually given credit for inventing paper (out of bark and hemp), the paper wasps really deserve this recognition.

Like the nest of the honeybee, a hornet's nest is strong enough to carry many times its own weight, even though the walls of the cells are less than one-tenth of a millimeter thick. Construction is a key to the nest's performance. A hornet's nest can be crumpled almost as easily as a page of newsprint, yet it can withstand a tremendous amount of downward tension without tearing apart, just as a sheet of notepaper can be crushed or torn but is very hard to pull apart. Once again, it is the cellulose in the plant fibers that provides the paper's great tensile strength. Another reason for the strength of a hornet's nest is that nothing heavier than hornet brood is ever stored there. While hornets relish the taste of nectar and stolen honey, they do not store it in their nest or feed it to their young. The brood is fed solely on animal protein.

While the wax cells of the honeybee's comb hang in vertical sheets and point outward and upward, the hexagonal paper cells of a hornet's nest open downward. The sheets of paper cells in a hornet's nest are built out laterally and arranged in as many as eight horizontal "tiers." The mass of tiered cells is then completely wrapped in a protective sheath of paper.

A new nest is started by the queen hornet herself. When she emerges in spring, she finds a sheltered tree limb or chooses the underside of a porch roof or other sturdy horizontal surface not likely to be disturbed. She hangs the first layer of eight or so hexagonal cells from a short overhead cord. This rudimentary group of cells looks somewhat like an umbrella that has been flipped inside out by the wind. She then lays the first of her many eggs in these "starter cells" to produce the workers she will soon need to help build the rest of the nest. Without her workers (and drones) she would accomplish little. Once the construction crew grows large enough, the queen relaxes and allows the workers to feed her and take over the remainder of the nest building.

The nest is built entirely of paper pulp and hornet saliva. Nothing more is needed, and the necessary raw materials are everywhere. The wood for commercial paper is boiled, washed, bleached, screened, beaten, screened again, and drained, and the fibers are mechanically agitated until they mat. The paper is then rolled and pressed in yet another set of machinery. Fillers are often used to increase the strength of the paper. The hornet eliminates most of these time-consuming steps. Worker hornets scrape small bundles of wood fibers off of old barnboards, tree trunks, clothespins, cardboard, old wicker furniture, fenceposts, and any other unpainted wood in the immediate vicinity, as well as dried weed and plant stems. (The sound of a hornet's mandibles scraping wood for pulp can be heard from more than a few feet away.) They then masticate the particles, mixing their saliva with the wood until it becomes a sticky wad of pulp.

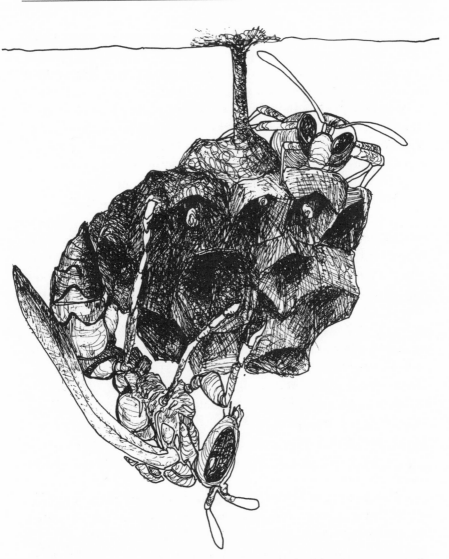

The queen "paper wasp," or bald-faced hornet, builds a starter nest of paper for the first of the workers she will raise to help her complete the nest.

When pulped, stretched, and dried out, the wood fibers become matted and strengthened just like the intermingled strands that can be seen in good bond writing paper. Each hornet carries its bundle of pulp back to the nest and incorporates it into the growing mass of brood cells by drawing out new cells, adding pulp to the rims of cells in progress, or pasting it onto the outer nest envelope.

A hornet shapes out a hexagonal cell by exerting pressure with its antennae around the inner surfaces of the cell walls. Once enough cells have been built and an egg has been stuck into each, the workers enclose the entire comb in a multilayered envelope of paper, patiently adding a strip of paper at a time to each layer. The striated sheath of a completed hornet's nest reveals a subtle pattern of overlapping grays and browns.

There are a couple of reasons for building multiple layers of paper around the nest of cells. The envelope helps to strengthen the nest and hold the tiers of cells in place. But more important, the air that is trapped between the layers of the outer envelope insulates the nest, which must be kept at a constant 86° F. for the developing larvae. If the temperature does drop, worker hornets gather about the outside of the nest to warm it up while the brood wriggle around inside their cells to help raise the temperature. When extra cells are needed for additional brood, the innermost layer of the envelope can be removed to build new cells outward from the old without disturbing the weather- and predator-proofing outer envelope. New exterior layers are added to the envelope as the interior layers are removed. A maturing hornet's nest always grows evenly from the inside out and maintains its overall globular proportions.

The papery nursery-fortress is nearly impregnable. The hornet's most persistent enemies, ants, can through their sheer numbers infiltrate and decimate many honeybee nests. For this reason, hornets build just one easily defended entrance at the very bottom of their nest.

Hornet larvae eat nothing but animal protein, and a significant source of that food—in addition to caterpillars, grubs, and the meat of small mammals—is the honeybee. Hornets will enter a honeycomb or kill off honeybees in midair and carry them back to the hornet brood. In fact, hornets are such a menace to honeybee hives that beekeepers always stay alert to their presence and destroy any hornets' nests they find anywhere near the apiary.

The bald-faced hornet builds a football-size nest of paper hexagonal cells surrounded by several more layers of paper processed by thousands of workers. Inside the nest, the brood hang upside down in their cells waiting to be fed. Once grown, they too will go afield and gather the wood fibers needed to build the nest.

Young hornets are packed into their cells like niblets on a cob of corn, their heads resting at the entrances of their downward-pointing cradles. This is the position from which each larva is fed. The workers always first sting and paralyze their prey and masticate it to pulp before feeding it to the young. When the hornet larva is ready to pupate and is no longer in need of food, it spins a cap of silk over its cell. Then, when the time comes to leave the nest, it chews through the silk cap and emerges from the cell to take on its duties as a new member of the colony. By winter the workers and drones of the present colony all die off, but a new colony will refill the nest come next spring.

TWELVE

The Potter Wasp's Earthen Vessel

T HE POTTER WASP, OR MASON WASP, IS ONE OF THE MOST agile builders in the insect kingdom. With its strong mandibles and forelegs, it can collect and shape dabs of mud or clay into perfect spheres, carry them back to its tiny adobe cell, and while hanging upside down in midair, lower the spheres of clay and work them into its nest before they can dry.

The potter wasp does not live in its remarkable little earthen cells. It builds them especially for its young. A typical solitary wasp, the potter wasp works and lives alone. During breeding season, it makes several tiny pottery vessels with bulbous bodies and narrow necks, one for each of its young. It collects wet clay or mud, or it mixes dry earth with water. The potter wasp begins each new nest with a flat base of clay, which it builds up, just as a human potter does, from many single pellets of clay until it has created a sturdy, weatherproof hollow form.

Each nest takes a couple of hours to build. The wasp's long, slender body and narrow waist—typical of all wasps—help give it the dexterity it needs to shape out the walls and narrow down the mouth of the vessel. It uses its whole body as it manipulates

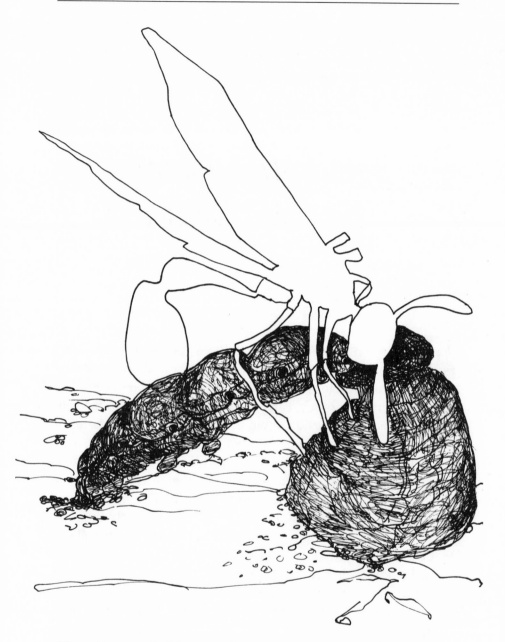

The potter wasp builds an earthen vessel for each of her young. So each will have food as soon as it is born, she stuffs each vessel with a live caterpillar and seals it up.

the wet pellets into a solid form. It must work quickly from all sides at once because the mud dries rapidly. The wasp also polishes the inner walls of the vessel using its head and flexible belly.

Now the potter wasp's tiny earthen chamber is more accurately a combination tomb and nursery, for when the adult wasp finishes each clay cell, it stuffs it with a live but paralyzed caterpillar or insect grub. It then lays an egg inside the vessel and seals it off with a final pellet of mud.

THIRTEEN

The Beaver's Watery Fortress

T HE BEAVER IS BORN TO BUILD. NOT VERY LONG AFTER IT first appears in its watery new world, the young beaver is apprenticed by its parents into a lifelong career of civil engineering. Born fully equipped with sharp incisors, thick protective fur, and a distinctive paddle-shaped tail, every young beaver is soon schooled in the art of felling trees and transporting them along with the branches, mud, stones, and debris that are used to build dams and erect the animal's famous dwelling, the beaver lodge. Once these rudimentary cutting and towing

The beaver's incisors, like those of all rodents, grow throughout its lifetime. It must use them often to keep them filed down, and this constant need to gnaw wood perfectly suits its continuing need to cut wood for building and repairing its dams and lodges.

skills have been passed on to the young by the older generation, the beaver's innate urge to cut wood, erect dams, and build lodges never disappears.

Even though it is North America's largest rodent by far (mature beavers weigh between 45 and 60 pounds, and some have been known to reach more than 100 pounds), the beaver is an extremely vulnerable animal. Although physically strong, it is tentative and slow moving on land and mild-mannered and cautious in temperament. The beaver seldom fights. In order to survive and protect itself from its traditional predators—fishers, coyotes, wolverines, otters, bears, and other carnivores—the beaver makes it a practice to work, eat, breed, play, and sleep within, above, or surrounded by water. It is a survival plan that has allowed *Castor canadensis* to exist, and usually to flourish, in absolutely every part of the country, from the Far North to the deserts of the Southwest.

Beavers are committed animals, both as mates and as builders. Once they finally choose a suitable site and begin building their dams and lodges, nothing short of a natural calamity or human intervention (if that) can persuade them to abandon their operation. Whether this inborn tenacity has to do with the care with which they choose a site or because they are, in a sense, building for their own future, beavers will not be budged. They will repair deliberately damaged dams and lodges night after night if necessary, giving up a site only if and when they run out of food, are killed, or are physically carted away. So determined are they to hold on to an area once they claim it, that beavers have been known to incorporate crowbars, railroad ties, and even the box traps meant to capture them into their dams.

At a fresh homesite—one chosen by a newly mated pair, for example—beavers always first build a dam. In a pinch, a pair of beavers can build a 2-foot-high, 10-foot-long dam in a couple of nights, but work usually proceeds much more carefully and with great discrimination. The woods around beaver colonies are filled with partially chewed trees or trees felled and left behind. Some have been gnawed for food, and some have been deemed too large to haul to the water, but many trees are chosen and then abandoned as unsuitable for one reason or another. Narrow streams and small ponds are most often selected as building sites because the food is usually more abundant there than it is around lakes and other large bodies of water.

Supported by its broad, flat tail, the beaver stands up while biting into a tree trunk. The animal's massive skull gives its chisel-like incisors tremendous cutting force. A beaver can lop off a 1/2-inch-thick sapling in one bite and sever a 6-inch aspen in ten to twenty minutes. (Some hard-working beavers have been known to cut down trees 50 inches in diameter, but the animal obviously has no use for lumber of this size. But since all rodents must constantly gnaw wood to keep their ever-growing

Beavers have been known to fell trees of great girth, either to get at the slender top branches or to keep their teeth filed down.

incisors from getting too long, this may be why trees are sometimes felled and abandoned.)

The beaver chips away at a tree until the tree begins to weaken and sway, then the animal runs for the safety of the water as the tree topples. First the interior bark, the twigs, and the leaves are stripped from the tree and eaten, then the branches are cut from the trunk and floated or hauled across the water. The beaver cuts larger trees into short, manageable lengths and rolls or pushes them to the water with its head or shoulder. But why use so much energy to fell trees when trees that have already fallen are so much lighter? Green wood is at least a third heavier than dead wood. Beavers invest so much time cutting fresh wood for their lodges because dead wood is brittle and rotten and cannot be bent and shaped as live wood can.

Beavers force sticks into the mud of the streambed to form the skeleton of the dam structure. Then mud, logs, grass, leaves, rocks, and anything and everything else that is available and movable are hauled down to the site and wedged into the frame of the dam. Beavers are amazingly strong animals and are capable of transporting their own weight in wood, rocks, and other dam-building materials. The beaver carries mud by packing it against its chest and holding on to it with its front paws. It can carry rocks (as well as an infant beaver) in its paws while "walking" nearly erect and using its tail for balance. Contrary to popular lore, the beaver does not use its broad tail to transport mud or slap mud like plaster onto its lodge and dam, although it no doubt would if it could manage to maneuver its tail this way.

Beavers always adapt their dam building to the prevailing water conditions. If the water is flowing more swiftly than the dam can sustain, spillways or passageways are sometimes built to carry off excess water until the pressure subsides or until the dam is strengthened. Sometimes smaller dams are built to lessen pressure on a main dam. While a dam is under construction, water is allowed to percolate through it until the dam is completely filled in and built up. The completed beaver dam is always much wider at the base than at the top and is tilted upstream against the force of the current. An average dam is about 6 feet high and 15 feet long, although a beaver dam fully 4,000 feet in length was once discovered in New Hampshire.

In large colonies housing several clans, all of the animals work constantly to maintain the dam, sometimes adding length, sometimes height, and always repairing damage caused by the current, rain or snow, their own activity, or other animals. The sound of water seems to stimulate beavers to build. Snowmelt and spring rains urge them out of their winter "slow season" to step up the pace to build new dams, to shore up existing dams, and to repair, enlarge, and renovate their lodges in anticipation of new family members. Smaller dams may have to be built upstream to reduce pressure on the main dam, and extra brooding space may have to be added to lodges to nurture new beaver kits.

Once a dam has slowed the current and broadened the beaver's food and supplies territory, work on the lodge begins. Sometimes simple shoreline lodges are built or excavated from the soil, but the classic beaver lodge is built in the center of the water. Building proceeds from the bottom up. Sticks are "planted" in the mud of the stream or pond bottom to form the base of the lodge, which will eventually need thousands of such sticks by the time the dome of the lodge rises above the water surface. As they work underwater during warm weather, northern beavers leave a supply of food branches on the stream or pond bed near the lodge so they can reach food in winter when the water freezes over. Thus they won't have to go far from the lodge or get stuck out on the ice while foraging for food in the dead of winter.

The medieval castles built nearly a thousand years ago had rounded masonry walls as thick as 80 feet and interior cores of loose stones and other rubble. The walls tapered inward as they rose, giving the castles stable bases and great resistance against battering rams and catapults. Mass, weight, and height gave these fortresses their tremendous strength and impenetrability. A beaver's lodge is built using similar principles: It has thick, sloping walls of rubble plastered over with a mortar of mud. It

Water is the beaver's main mode of living. It floats food and building materials across water broadened by its dams, and it builds its famous "castle" lodge completely surrounded by a protective moat of deep water.

is designed to withstand a great deal of battering from within as well as without.

While building the lodge, beavers swim a steady relay from the growing mound to the woods to gather building materials. Unsteady and slow on land, beavers move through water with the grace, speed, and dexterity of otters. The beaver's anatomy is marvelously adapted to its nearly full-time aquatic existence. Its broad, flattened tail consists of cartilage and bone and is covered with thick scales. The beaver uses its tail to steer and propel itself through the water. When it slaps its tail on the water in anger or fear, the message can be heard for more than a mile away. It uses its hind feet, which have webbing between the toes, to propel it along while it holds its small front paws curled close to its chest to help reduce drag.

Since the bulk of the lodge rests below the water, much of the building goes on beneath the water's surface. Materials are not simply dumped onto the mound. Sticks, rocks, and mud have to be placed together with care. Because of its large lung capacity, the beaver is able to stay below water for as long as fifteen minutes if necessary, time enough to do a good deal of work on dams and lodges and maybe feed on underwater vege-

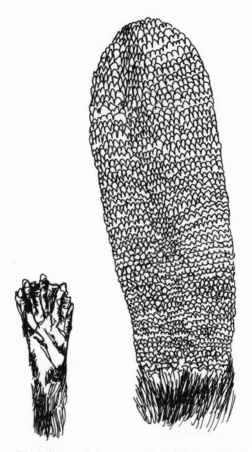

The beaver's webbed feet and heavy, paddlelike tail propel it through the water with grace and power. The mother beaver often uses her tail to protect her newborn kits from the cold, and a slap of the tail against the water surface warns intruders not to come too close.

tation. Its eyes are protected by a thin, transparent membrane that allows it to see what it is doing and where it is going without sustaining eye damage. Its nose and ears are equipped with valves that automatically seal off those organs each time the beaver dives into the water.

Sticks, leaves, twigs, mud, rocks, and other debris from the pond or stream bottom are heaped onto the growing lodge mound until it rises above the water. Although beavers will build or excavate lodges at the shoreline, it is the mound or "castle" type lodge surrounded by a "moat" of water that makes for the best protection against predators. The mound that rises above the surface of the water is plastered with mud until it becomes airtight and watertight, except for the very peak of the mound, which is left open to provide ventilation for the interior sleeping and feeding chambers. (In cold weather, beaver breath sometimes can be seen rising from a lodge like smoke from a tepee.)

For centuries, human builders around the world have applied mudlike stucco in thin layers to help stabilize their houses. These buildings last for centuries, in part because, unlike rigid masonry, the stucco adjusts to minor shifts caused by changes in the weather. Because the stucco is weaker than the underlying structure, it easily adapts itself to movement by forming fine, hairline cracks without falling apart as the building shifts. Mud works in the same fashion on a beaver lodge, providing weather resistance and exterior resilience. And similar to human builders, beavers continually add fresh mud to fill in the cracks caused by erosion.

The beaver lodge is highly resistant to the pressures of wind and snow, as well. A roof is always more vulnerable than the walls in high winds, because the juncture between walls and roof is the weakest point in the structure. And a large roof collapses easily under the weight of heavy snows. A beaver's conical lodge easily resists both elements, because roof and walls are one.

The finished lodge mound will be about 15 feet across and rise about 5 feet above the water, although some older beaver lodges, expanded and repaired over many years, may reach as much as 25 feet across. Once the mound, or "superstructure," is in place, the beavers then dive below the water and methodically tunnel their way into the interior of the mound. Using their sharp incisors and forepaws, they chew and dig several tunnels into the lodge from below the water's surface. They then dig out hollow chambers within the top of the lodge, above the water level. Two spaces are cleared out. The beaver uses the first space, located a few inches above the water level, as a place to eat and drain off excess water from its fur. A second space, located about a foot above the first, is layered with finely shredded wood and is used for sleeping, resting, and rearing the kits, which will nurse here with their mother until they are ready to leave the lodge. These tiered or stacked chambers reduce the overall weight of the roof, making it much less likely to cave in.

Beaver lodges are remarkably warm, even in the most frigid weather. Some materials conduct heat quickly and others slowly, and slow is always better. A layer of still air provides the best insulation, and the next best insulator is dense, fibrous matter. A thick enough layer of matter will reduce the loss of heat into and out of a dwelling, and wood fibers make extremely good thermal insulators. It is the moving air currents that whisk away warmth and bring in the cold, and the shredded and woven organic matter that forms the walls of the beaver lodge traps the air and keeps it still. Warm air generated by the animals' bodies tends to cling to each strand of woody fiber within the shell of the lodge.

Beavers often dig "canals" from the shoreline back into the woods. Though the dam naturally expands their forage area by flooding it with water, they sometimes have to range farther afield for food and building materials. Leaving little to chance, the beavers also use these canals as escape hatches. If a beaver encounters a fisher, coyote, or other predator while foraging or cutting trees, it has a direct pathway back to the safety of the lodge.

Once the beaver is in the water or inside its lodge, few of its natural enemies can reach it. In cold weather, the mud-plastered exterior of the lodge becomes nearly as hard and impenetrable as stone. At other times, the beaver may actually be safer in the water than it is in its own lodge. Water-going predators such as the otter, equally comfortable and skilled in the water, have been known to enter beaver lodges through the underwater tunnels.

Large beaver colonies of five or six adults and their young are operated almost like compounds. When several beaver clans of primary and extended families decide to stay together

The underwater entrance to a beaver's lodge is protection enough against all predators except for the otter, which is as agile in the water as the beaver. Sticks are "planted" in the bed of a lake or pond just outside the lodge entrance for winter feeding.

in a particularly abundant area, the bulk of their efforts often goes into maintaining control of their "fortress." A large, cooperative colony of beavers will work almost constantly to maintain its dams and lodges and to keep intruding beavers out of its lodges and feeding grounds.

Beaver social law dictates that the female select the homesite and provide the social stability and continuity for the whole clan. If her mate dies, she will stay on and take a new mate. But if the female should die, her mate will usually leave the area. The beaver family shares all dam and lodge maintenance work, foraging, and territorial defense. When young beavers are about two years old, they head not far downstream to find their own site. Sometimes one of the juveniles will inherit the parental lodge.

Beaver kits are born and weaned inside the topmost chamber of the lodge, where they remain safe against the elements and predators until they are old enough to enter the water and learn the parents' lodge- and dam-building trades.

At the close of the last century, the North American beaver population was almost eradicated both by trappers for its luxurious fur and by farmers because it was considered a nuisance. In this century, the beaver flourishes once again, but there still exists a bias against the animal for what it does naturally: flood land, along with whatever happens to exist there, including railroad tracks, roads, and pastures. What many do not realize is that while beavers can cause damage, they can also bring many benefits. In places where beavers decide to build dams and lodges, their unceasing labors often increase the overall quality of river water, plant life, and wildlife.

FOURTEEN

The Deer Yard

HOOVED ANIMALS ARE NOT KNOWN FOR CONSTRUCTING anything more than the most rudimentary nest for shelter and breeding, and yet our most common and adaptable deer, the whitetail *(Odocoileus virginianus)*, happens to be an excellent landscaper. Unlike migrating western cousins such as elk and antelope, the white-tailed deer spends most of its life in one place and becomes intensely familiar with its 40- to 200-acre home territory. The whitetail herd works together to modify its home environment to provide for food, shelter, and protection against predators that share the deer's habitat largely because the whitetails are there.

White-tailed deer herds gradually develop amazingly intricate networks of trails that radiate from the main deer yard across acres of forest and meadow. They use these trails for traveling to distant forage sites in winter and as emergency escape routes from predators such as wolves, coyotes, lynx, bobcats, and domestic dogs. Whitetails "follow the leader" in hardpacking a trail, and within a short time the entire herd memorizes all of the main trail routes as well as the smaller interlocking crossover and "subroutes" throughout the entire system. In summer, these well-traveled trails are soon denuded of all edible vegetation, so the deer cannot use them for foraging; instead, they travel along these trails to more distant feeding sites, breaking fresh trails as they forage.

Some white-tailed deer trail networks have been in use for decades, but new offshoots are made throughout the year, especially if all of the green browse in the winter yard has disappeared. Whitetails may keep to a fixed pattern of movement along their trail systems for weeks at a time, trying not to go beyond their familiar routes in order to avoid getting caught off guard in ravines, thick vegetation, or other strange and unsafe spots. In some heavily hunted areas, whitetails even seem to know when to abandon popular but vulnerable and exposed routes and head for the hills until the hunters have gone.

Whitetails bed down in shallow "deer scrapes," 2-foot-long oval depressions that the deer scrape out with their hooves.

By the time a deep winter is well under way, the permanent bedding spots that white-tailed deer retire to each night often become many degrees warmer than the outer air. During a severe blizzard, the deer may be forced to stay in their beds for several days, yet they emerge warm and rested.

Whitetails also pack down familiar "runways," known to each member of the herd, which allow them to speed along the most direct route to the safety of the yard in times of trouble. Deer always take the paths of least resistance in creating their trails, winding them around swamps, downfalls, boulders, and briar patches. Long trails are made close to the shore around lakes, bogs, and along riverbanks. Deer trails snake without apparent purpose all over the forest, but the whitetails know all of the shortcuts to emergency hiding places along the trails and which offshoots connect with the main trails.

An individual whitetail often makes its own brief side trails fingering out from the main trail; these lead to secret spots where it can browse or rest while watching out for predators. Deer trails also are interlaced so that "last chance" escape routes that are known to the whole herd can easily be found. Often when one deer, perhaps injured, is temporarily separated from the herd, the rest of the herd will wait for it on one of these routes.

Some deer trails are used only in summer and some only in winter. In summer, "loitering grounds" are often stamped out in an open, sunny meadow or in a cleared area inside the woods near the main feeding grounds. This is a safe area where deer can congregate and chew their cuds before going back into the forest to forage or before bedding down to sleep or rest. A whitetail loitering area is easy to detect by the hundreds of hoof tracks stamped into the earth and dotted with dung heaps.

During extreme winters in the Northeast, whitetails "yard up" within dense, warm stands of evergreens, taking advantage whenever possible of a southern exposure, to seek shelter from four months or so of extreme cold and harsh winds. Whitetails generally stay in small groups of fewer than a dozen, but in times of severe weather a greater number of white-tailed deer than usual may yard up together for the season. When this happens, all of the deer must become familiar with the designated sleeping arrangements within the yard and the complicated trail network of the "host" herd, as well as the trail system's overlapping forage and escape routes branching out from the main yard.

*During hard winters, a larger group of whitetails may "yard up"
beneath thick stands of evergreens and leave the warmth and shelter
of the yard only to forage for food. When the weather becomes warm,
the deer stamp out "loitering grounds" in an open meadow or
clearance in the woods where they congregate to chew their cuds.*

The whitetail's trail system branches outward from the main yard and takes an erratic course throughout the woods, twisting and turning around obstacles and looping over itself. The deer use these trails to travel to foraging areas and as quick-escape routes when fleeing from predators.

White-tailed deer sleep in "forms," or depressions, near or under brush or below overhanging evergreen boughs. After much use, these deer beds often come to resemble small dens, and throughout the winter months the same deer will use the same bed over and over, much like a group of students in an open dormitory. The air in a well-used deer bed is often much warmer than the outer temperatures, and the deer will emerge after a heavy blizzard or deep freeze surprisingly warm and

When they stick to their well-traveled system of trails, white-tailed deer can safely forage for food and quickly escape back to the yard in times of trouble without floundering in the deep snow.

rested. During an especially heavy snowfall, when the trails are impassable, the deer will sometimes stay in their beds for a few days before going out to break the trails. Sometimes, however, in severe below-zero weather, deer will have to leave their beds in the middle of the night and move along their trails just to stay warm and alive.

In order to survive a harsh northern winter, a whitetail absolutely must stay out of the deep snow. If it is caught alone by a dog, coyote, or other predator in more than a foot or so of snow, it will easily flounder and collapse because of its small hooves. This is a frequent danger for pregnant females, which may have eaten little during a food-scarce winter. Yet all throughout the winter months, whitetails must go farther and farther from the relative safety of their yard in search of food. Their snow-packed network of familiar trails allows them to move quickly and safely in search of food while using the least possible amount of energy. During blizzards, a memorized trail system is a lifesaver when deer are foraging far away from the warmth of the yard and the herd. But at the same time, too many hardpacked deer trails are a bad sign to biologists, who know that the presence of long, oft-used trails during a given winter reflects a dangerous scarcity of food.

PART THREE

Innovative Weavers

I N WEAVING, THE WORD *SETT* REFERS TO THE NUMBER OF threads in an inch made up by the warp and weft. It determines the balance and, more important, the strength of the textile. Warp and weft, of course, give all fabrics their height and breadth and great resilience, whether the material is woven of silk, hemp, wool, or cotton. All natural fibers have great elasticity and even greater tensile strength, but when woven or matted together, they may easily match the carrying loads of wood or earth.

Whenever elastic materials are woven together, they also gain tremendous strength in proportion to their weight. Hammocks, baskets, and rope bridges all can carry a huge load without breaking or permanently sagging. This lightweight elasticity gives the silk of a spider's web and the grass pouch of an oriole's nest tremendous strength under considerable strain, allowing them to rebound to their former shapes after being stressed. Where stiffer, less yielding material might snap under the weight of a mother oriole and her eggs or from the thrashing of a snared bumblebee in a spider's web, these two organic materials simply go with the load.

The protein in silk and the cellulose in plant fibers are what give these two substances their tremendous plasticity and high tensile strength. When stretched they do not deform but snap back to their original shapes. Like the iron and steel that builders began using in the nineteenth century in the place of heavy and unstable stones and brick, silk and plant fibers are light, cheap, and plentiful.

Of course, birds usually combine different strengthening techniques in a single nest. Tension *and* compression are achieved when flexible twigs are combined with the strong, rigid properties of dry mud or clay. When mud or clay is mixed with grass or saliva, it takes on the strength and sealing abilities of the best plasters and mortars, which also provide both compression and tension. When the hummingbird weaves spider's silk into the slender plant fibers of its nest, it is combining the tensile strength of wood and of silk, as well as the sticky binding properties of the silk. The hummingbird's nest, which is about the size of half a walnut shell, withstands rain, wind, and a couple of active chicks without falling apart or dropping off the twig it is glued to. The stickleback fish, which uses saliva in the construction of its nest of woven plant stems, achieves both tension and compression when the saliva hardens to a dense, rubberlike substance in the water.

To cut down on the cost of time and transport, human builders always try to use locally available materials whenever possible, and they hire workers who are expert at working with a particular building material. Masons are not called in to do carpentry work, and plumbers don't pour foundations. And no one shows up on the work site without the proper building tools. Likewise, an animal's strength, construction skills, and tools, and the local availability of materials all determine what kind of shelter the animal will build.

A bird has only so much time and energy at its disposal in which to build its nest. It must find a mate; search for building materials; lay the eggs; feed, protect, and rear the young; and then, if it is a migrator, fly south for the winter with a healthy brood in tow. If it spends too much energy foraging for scarce nesting materials, it depletes the strength it needs to forage for food and feed the young, placing itself as well as its brood in jeopardy. Birds need food as well as a nest in order to stay warm and alive, so the bird always uses materials that are light enough to carry back to the building site in its beak or feet. And since the most energy-consuming activity for a bird is flight, it must find those materials close by.

The building material of the orb-weaving spider is contained within its very anatomy. The spider has more or less cornered the market on silk production, so the presence of spiders is essential to the livelihood of the hummingbird, which uses more silk than any other bird in the construction of its nest. The spider's anatomical "tools" and physical strength could not handle any building material other than silk, so this is what it uses. Just as the engineer Gustave Eiffel had precise, unfailing building plans for the construction of his tower, bridges, and buildings of iron gridwork, so the spider has a web-weaving formula that works time and again. The garden spider even destroys and reconstructs its webs over and over, much as Manhattan's steel-framed skyscrapers are erected and demolished within a few years' time. And the spider, too, in a sense is dependent upon locally available building supplies. Since the spider's silk is composed largely of protein, it must have a large supply of insects to trap and eat in order to produce the silk it needs to build its web.

Most birds are incapable of lifting, let alone manipulating, materials other than those that they use in their nests. There simply aren't any available materials lighter than twigs, moss, feathers, and grass. Since a bird's building tools consist of its beak, feet, and body, the materials it uses must be light, flexible, and most of all, abundant.

The local flora and fauna of the area in which an animal breeds also determines the specific kinds of materials it will use in its home. Birds of the same species from different parts of the country usually build very similar nests, but the materials they use in their nests differ depending on their location. Timing comes into play, too. The crucial vegetation that goes into a bird's nest often comes from plants that are emerging just as migrating birds are arriving for the breeding season. These plants are always on the birds' list of standard building supplies for a particular locale. If a traditional nest-building material should suddenly vanish from the landscape, the birds would no doubt find a successful substitute, and that material would quickly become traditional.

During the last century, most birds wove horsehair into their nests. It was found everywhere, and it possessed some highly recommended nest-building features: strength, length, resilience, and weavability. Once the automobile was invented, however, horses became less numerous and birds could no longer find horsehair as easily. Since few things can quite match the usefulness of horsehair for nest building, nothing has really taken its place, although most birds will add colored yarn to their nests if it is placed outside for them.

Birds are the most eccentric and creative of all builders. They are not as daunted as other animals by the presence of humans: Our cities and suburbs frequently have more nesting birds per square mile than nearby rural areas. In fact, birds are fascinated by human sources of building materials, and if they can lift something useful and fly it back to their nests, they will. Perhaps because of their mobility, birds can range farther and wider than many other animals in search of new, improved, and interesting items for their homes.

FIFTEEN

Weavers Extraordinaire

B IRDS NEST ALMOST ANYWHERE: ON AND BELOW THE ground, inside tree hollows, on the surface of water, on moving boats and trains—even on a working steam shovel. But most creatures of the air prefer to breed and live up there as well. This is where most find their food and, more important, protection from predators while roosting and raising their young. Imagine, though, the construction challenges faced in such an unstable environment: The nest's foundation constantly shifts in the slightest breeze, is lashed to and fro by violent windstorms, and is periodically soaked by heavy rains. What is more, materials that are the lightest and closest at hand must be used to construct the nest, all with the greatest economy of effort and in a short period of time.

A bird's most common nest-building problems are finding and transporting the right building materials, anchoring the nest to an awkward surface, and then fusing the materials into a shape that will shelter the eggs and then the young until they fledge. And the birds must do all of this without exhausting themselves; otherwise, they would not be able to feed and care for their young.

Still, the energy consumed in building a nest is daunting. Many birds easily make more than a thousand flights to build a single nest for a single breeding season. Since flying is by far the most energy-consuming activity for a bird, once the materials are gathered and transported, work on the nest itself takes far less effort. This is one reason why wire, cotton, string, paper, fiberglass, and even cement are often found in bird nests. If an artificial material is close by and if it works as well as a natural item, a bird will not hesitate to incorporate it into its nest. For example, a warbler's nest found in California consisted of nothing but Kleenex. A raven's nest in Texas was made entirely of barbed wire; the usual sticks were not available and the bird had no time to lose. And again in California, office workers found, perched on a building beam, a nest built by a pair of canyon wrens from paper clips, rubber bands, matches, pins, shoelaces, thumbtacks and other office supplies—and no natural materials. The nest was eight inches high and weighed more than 2 pounds.

The bulk of a typical bird nest, however, usually contains time-proven natural building materials. The young must be insulated from the cold or they will die, and only plant materials can provide this protection. For their weight and construction purposes, twigs, grass stems, and shredded bark are as strong, flexible, and durable as steel. Mud or the silk of spiderwebs and insect cocoons make bonds strong enough to hold a nest fast to a tree branch or a cliff face even in the highest winds. And fine feathers, human hair, animal fur, and the down of thistle and milkweed are as soft and cushioning and warm as the highest-rated man-made insulation.

Protein is the strengthening compound common to all of these organic nest-building materials. Silk, for example, is strong and elastic. Birds either stretch it out into a single strand and weave it into the plant material as a mortar for the nest or use it as a binder to fasten the nest to a tree branch. The cellulose of green vegetation and wood is an excellent load-bearing material that also happens to be insoluble in water and extremely lightweight. It is flexible yet has great tensile strength for its weight. This is why wood is still used in almost all homes. What is more, cellulose fibers become stronger still when wet.

Once built, all bird nests must hold up under the weight of the eggs and young, the parent birds, and the weather, and this they do very well. Even large nests that crash to the ground from great heights usually land intact. The weight of the twigs alone helps hold them together, but it is the skillful way in which birds weave them, using binders and fasteners such as thorns, saliva, mud, and cobwebs, that keeps nests intact. Also, the center of a cup nest is more densely woven of smaller twigs, providing a firm support to the slightly more malleable, larger-twigged walls.

Most birds will test out potential nest sites before building. Robins and other cup builders gauge the circumference of a site by pivoting in the forks of different tree limbs to get a feeling for the space. Some male birds, such as wrens and warblers, build "dummy nests" to attract a female, usually unlined and ill-conceived masses of sticks. If a female takes over the nest she either renovates it or tosses it out and starts over. Some small birds opt for safety first and choose to nest in the lower parts of the nests of large birds. Kestrels and kingbirds may nest inside the nests of golden eagles, while grackles and house sparrows sometimes seek shelter in osprey nests. The little birds gain automatic protection from the big birds as well as their left-overs.

Swifts use a sticky, mucuslike saliva to bind the feathers and plant pieces of their nests together. It dries to a rubbery sub-stance that strengthens as well as waterproofs the nest. Swift saliva is all that holds an entire nest to the vertical surfaces of a cave or wall. Thrushes cement the woven grasses of their nests so firmly with mud that many generations of birds can be raised in the same nest. The nests of cliff swallows are adhered with nothing more than mud to the vertical walls of cliffs, and the house martin's nest also is attached with mud to walls. The bushtit of the West painstakingly separates the silken threads of insect cocoons and spiderwebs to weave and bind its nest mate-rials together. Essentially, whichever nest materials, whether artificial or organic, work for a particular bird will be used again and again until something better comes along.

Many materials may be used in a single bird nest. The small prairie warbler's cup nest has an outer shell of milkweed and fleabane daisy cemented with insect silk; a middle layer of plant down, feathers, and hair; and an inner lining of soft grass tops. Seven distinct items are combined for structural strength, insulation, waterproofing, and warmth, and all must be gathered from the same general area within about a week, in time to cradle the freshly laid eggs. The nest is held in place on a slender tree branch by nothing more than silken threads.

Like all cup-nest builders, the prairie warbler first selects an anchor spot on a branch or twigs. She smears the silk onto the branch with her beak, then uses her belly and breast to press plant fibers onto the branch to create the base of the nest, taking the loose fibrous ends of the plants and pressing them into the silk to anchor the nest base. Next she builds up the walls of the nest from the inside, using all of her body as her building tools. Breast, throat, belly, half-raised wings, and feet are all used to weave, shape, and pack down the inside and the outer walls of the nest. She pivots inside the nest as she works. This is how all cup nests get their round shapes.

Bird nests are a remarkable combination of economy, materials, size, and strength. Every bird nest reflects the needs and capacities of its builder, from the 1-inch, 1-ounce cup nest of the hummingbird to the 10-foot, 1-ton platform nest of the bald eagle.

The Oriole's Hanging Pouch

In late fall and winter, when the leaves are gone from the trees, the pendulous nests of orioles can be seen dangling from tree limbs like so many lost knitted socks. Orioles build their pouch nests as high up as they can, anywhere from 6 to 30 feet above the ground and well out of harm's way. Female orioles do the nest building. They weave their surprisingly sturdy nests of plant fibers, hair, string, and other long strands of material, including colored yarn, and fill them with a loose lining of wool, hair, and fine grasses.

The oriole's signature swinging pouch looks roughly the same all across the country, but the materials different orioles use vary as much as the local landscape. The black-headed oriole of Texas makes a tiny, 3-inch-long pouch of dry woven grasses. It hangs its nest within dense mesquite trees or

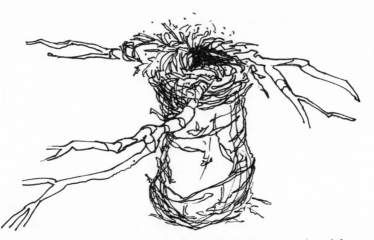

The oriole's pendulous nest hangs high above the ground and far out on the tip of a slender tree branch, where it is safe from all predators. Often the nests are hung directly over busy roadways. The pouch is so finely woven that it can withstand the wind and rain of several seasons.

bushes, attaching the sides and rim or opening of the nest to small branches and twigs. The Baltimore, or northern, oriole weaves a gray pouch that is twice as long as the little Texan oriole nest and suspends it by the rim from the narrow, drooping branches of maples, elms, poplars, conifers, and orchard trees, often directly above busy highways.

In the West, the Bullock's oriole makes an oval woven bag the same length as the Baltimore's but usually hangs it from the branches of cottonwoods, birches, willows, sycamores, and junipers 6 to 15 feet off the ground. This oriole weaves its nest of fine bark fibers and lines it with horsehair, plant down, wool, and mosses.

The hooded oriole of the Southwest makes a cuplike nest sewn with the fine fibers of palmetto leaves, yuccas, Spanish moss, or mistletoe and suspends it in sycamores, mesquite, and hackberry bushes. Scott's oriole, also of the Southwest, builds the nest walls of yucca leaf fibers and grasses and lines it with cotton batting and horsehair, and hangs the small, cuplike nest in the leaves of yuccas.

A female oriole begins construction of her nest with a long strand of fibers looped around the tip of a branch. This small swing will eventually become the nest entrance at the top of the pouch. She then pulls the loop parallel to two or more horizontal twigs and binds it to them with more fibers. Next she gathers and weaves more long fibers into the loop until it begins to lengthen. She now works from inside the tube, knitting new fibers into the growing "sock" until the fibers are crisscrossed and matted together, then finally "sews" the bottom together and crawls back up to the opening. She does not weave the lining together as other birds do but scatters the bottom of the pouch with soft, loose material. When the eggs are laid, this loose lining will help cushion them and keep them from smacking into one another and breaking as the pouch swings in the wind.

Swallows and Swifts: Aerial Architects

Swallows are sleek, glossy birds with wide, gaping mouths that are designed to scoop hundreds of insects out of the air in a single day. Their small, weak legs and feet make them clumsy and awkward on the ground, but they are in their element when soaring through the air. Swallows are colonizers, and scores of mating pairs can be found nesting together in a single location.

Before humans ever learned how to build, barn swallows were building their nests on the sheer vertical faces of cliffs and beneath steep, sheltered ledges along streams. Now most swallows prefer to colonize our buildings. Barn swallows make a small, neat, compact nest cup of mud or clay pellets mixed with straw and lined with feathers or horsehair. They plaster these small nests against either horizontal or vertical surfaces, and at the height of the breeding season as many as thirty pairs of barn swallows may inhabit a single building.

Cliff swallows originally nested in the wild as well, on bluff walls, in canyons, and in deep mountain gorges. Although some still nest in natural areas, as some barn swallows still do, cliff swallows prefer rough, vertical walls under the eaves of buildings, the undersides of bridges, and other human structures. More builders than weavers, they mold their stout, flask-shaped nests entirely out of mud or clay pellets that both sexes carry back to the work site in their mouths. The nests are lined

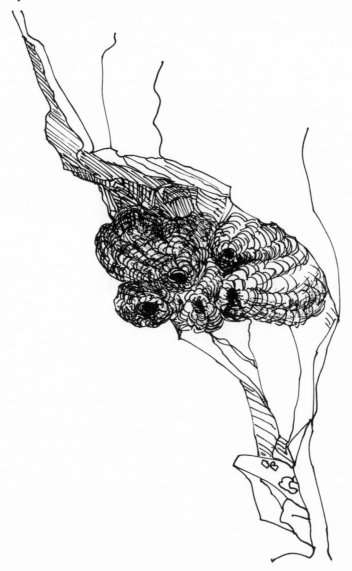

Cliff swallows build their vessel-shaped nests out of mud and clay. They carry the mud back to the nest sites in their mouths.

with feathers and grasses, and there is a small entrance to one side of the flask, sometimes ending in a narrow, protruding neck.

Our swiftest-flying small birds look like swallows but are not closely related to them. The swifts also have streamlined bodies and wide, gaping mouths for catching insects. Their tiny legs are so weak that they sometimes cannot get aloft again after landing on the ground. This is rarely a problem, however. These highly social birds live out their entire lives in the air, eating, mating, and building their nests. Some swifts have been known to spend the night on the wing high in the air instead of roosting on a solid surface. Chimney swifts nest on the vertical walls of chimneys, barns, and silos, and on rock walls. They must do a lot of clinging while building their nests and feeding their young, so their claws are particularly strong. They snap off small nest-building twigs with their feet while in flight, then weave and cement them together. They affix their cuplike nests to walls with their viscous, gluelike saliva.

The Tunneling Kingfisher

The kingfisher is found throughout the country, always near water. About a foot long, it has a bill as large and powerful looking as a woodpecker's and a distinctive raggedy crest. Its body appears smallish in comparison with its large head and crest. Its striking blue-white coloring and wide white collar make it unmistakable. The kingfisher spends most of its time perched above a stream- or riverbank. When it spots a fish, it dives straight down into the water.

When the time comes to breed, a pair of kingfishers burrow a long, tunneling nest into the sand, clay, or gravel banks of a river or creek. One bird could not do the work alone. Depending on the density of the soil, it can take a pair a few days to two or three weeks to finish the nest. The kingfishers use their strong feet and bills to excavate a 3- to 7-foot-long burrow ending in a rounded nest chamber 6 to 10 inches wide. The pair line the nursery with clean fish bones and fish scales, and the burrow is carefully hidden near the top of the bank beneath heavy vegetation.

Kingfishers work as a pair, using their beaks and feet to excavate protected nesting burrows deep inside the banks of streams and rivers.

The Eagle's Massive Platform Nest

Our largest birds of prey build the most imposing nests for their young. The bald eagle is more than a yard long and has a wingspan of 6 to 7 feet, and its massive platform nest matches its great size in every way, measuring as much as 8 feet across and 10 to 20 feet deep. The nest always has a commanding, unobstructed view of the surrounding area and is built in the tallest available tree 10 to 150 feet above the earth.

Eagles, which are believed to mate for life, develop a strong attachment to their traditional nesting sites. Many favorite nests are renovated and used by the same family for more than thirty years. Each year the eagles add on new material until the nest becomes deeper and deeper, heavier and heavier. Many nests eventually become so heavy—up to a couple of tons—that they break the very tree they are built in and crash to the ground.

To gather fresh sticks and branches for their nests, eagles may push down on tree branches until they break off, then carry them back to the nest in their feet. Eagles loosely stack the large sticks and branches of their nests, relying on the sheer

Eagles build their massive stick platform nests high up in the tallest trees or on the tops of cliffs, from which they can survey the area for signs of prey. The nests are often used for many generations and sometimes become so heavy that they break the tree.

weight of the wood to hold the nest together much like a brush pile becomes densely matted and packed as it grows in size.

The nest's broad, flattened stick foundation is lined with whatever loose material is available—pine needles, moss, grass, feathers, old bones, discarded clothing, cow and horse dung, and fur. Virtually anything will do. The nests of small songbirds may be tossed in for good measure. Fortunately, songbirds mate later than eagles; otherwise their eggs would no doubt end up in the eagle's nest lining as well.

The stunning bronze-gold of the golden eagle's crown and nape feathers give it its common name, but its scientific name— *Aquila chrysaetos*—means King of the Birds. The golden eagle is far more numerous in the West and Southwest, although there are small pockets of goldens living in New England and in the Adirondack Mountains of New York. It builds a similar huge platform nest of sticks and branches in conifers or directly on the tops of cliffs, from which it can survey the surrounding grasslands for prey.

Neither eagle camouflages its nest, even though the golden's is often built directly on the ground. Ironically, considering the work eagles put into their nests, both birds lay just two eggs per breeding season. And of these two chicks, only one is likely to survive, because the larger chick frequently pushes the weaker one out of the nest.

The Hummingbird's Invisible Cradle

The broad-tailed hummingbird of the Rocky Mountains nests in willows, aspens, alders, and cottonwoods. The female builds her 1- or 2-inch nest of spiderwebs and plant down, and camouflages it with chips of lichen and bark. The nest is nearly impossible to see, not only because of its miniature size, but also because the bird places it within dense foliage under over-

Hummingbirds build the smallest nests—tiny, 1-inch cups that blend in with the twigs and leaves of a tree. The cups are meticulously "shingled" with bits of lichen and spider's silk to strengthen the nest and help camouflage it.

hanging boughs. When she has finished building, she fills her nest with two pea-size eggs.

East of the Mississippi, the ruby-throated hummingbird nests in apple trees, beeches, and birches. The female constructs her nest of fern down, milkweed, thistles, and oak leaves on a twig or small branch, and obscures it on the outside with lichens and mosses. When the nest is built in an old apple tree that is lichen covered itself, it is impossible to detect. It resembles nothing more than a bole or other irregularity of the tree. The nest materials are meticulously bound together with a great deal of spider silk. In fact, the ruby-throated hummer often gets trapped in the spiderweb she is trying to harvest for her nest.

Both hummingbirds are fiercely protective of their broods and have been known to dart after birds as large as hawks that come too close to the hummers' nests.

SIXTEEN

The Orb Weaver's Silken Sculpture

THE COMMON GARDEN SPIDER BELONGS TO A GROUP OF arachnids famous for their remarkable orb webs. Although at first glance it appears to be a simple structure, the orb web, which is constructed by the female, actually is the end result of a tremendous amount of skill, resourcefulness, and foresight. A member of the Araneidae family, the female garden spider is her own small textile factory. Her tiny architectural achievement combines great flexibility and strength. The web shifts in the wind without snapping or distorting, and it performs its various functions beautifully. A large portion of her stomach is given over to the storage and production of silk, a protein that is both manufactured from and replenished by the prey she captures in her ingenious web.

Equipped with a half dozen pairs of glands connected to silk-ejecting "spinnerets" on her stomach, the spider can select the exact grade of silk needed for web weaving, locomotion, and ensnaring prey. The sum of life as she knows it is played out entirely on her two-dimensional geometric home. She builds a new web at least once a day and more often if it is damaged or destroyed. In fact, the garden spider can create a fresh orb web in just one or two hours.

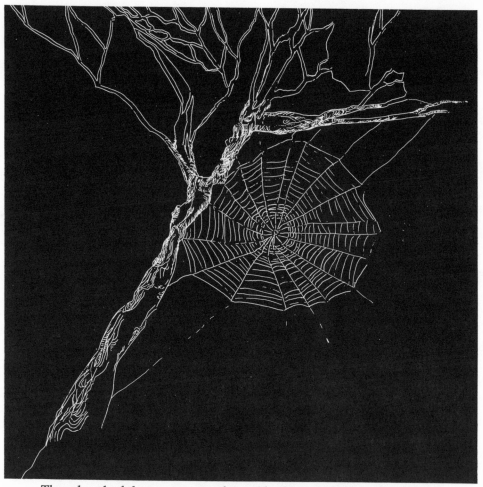

The orb web of the common garden spider is an architectural marvel.
So fine and lightweight that it is barely visible even to the prey it is
designed to catch, the silken structure can withstand wind, rain, and
even the thrashings of insects much larger than the spider itself.

She first sets up a "bridge" line from one object to another, tossing out a length of silk from her perch on a twig or leaf. This first line is critical, as it stabilizes the entire web and is often used over and over as the base for new webs. If she times things just right, the initial bridge line is picked up by an errant breeze and floated to the other side. If not, she reels it back, digests it, and tosses out a new line. (Some garden spiders "walk" their bridge line from one side to the other and anchor it at both ends.) When the line finally catches, the spider crawls across the bridge, backtracking a few times to thicken the line. At the halfway point, she drops to the ground with a new line and secures this end to the ground. This might be called her plumb line. She uses it like a tiny elevator to hoist herself up and down as she works. The web now has three spokes in place and looks much like the letter Y. The intersection of the Y forms the "hub" of the web. It is from this center of operations that the garden spider later conducts her business—waiting for prey.

Next she builds the outer frame of the web, moving about like a mountain climber, raising and lowering herself on her own silken lines and anchoring and pulling the lines taut as needed. She grasps and cuts lines using small claws and bristles at the ends of her legs. When the outer frame is completed, she adds the spokes, which radiate from the center hub, or "lookout," to the web's outer frame. Next she weaves in the prey-catching spiral. To avoid getting trapped in her own glue-coated threads, she first weaves a temporary spiral around the spokes using dry thread. She uses this rough "scaffold" as a surface upon which to move while carefully adding the more finely woven permanent sticky spiral. She then efficiently cuts away and eats the temporary dry spiral lines as she works. This used dry silk will be redigested and used again to shore up this web or to build a new one. Nothing is wasted.

She might weave together a small cache of leaves at the edge of the web and retreat there, where she will be safe from the weather and predators. But most often she takes up her position at the hub, which is separated from the sticky spiral by a brief "free zone" where she can move around without being hampered. Here she lies upside down in wait, her head pointed down toward the ground, for a sign of prey.

While waiting she keeps one leg on a spoke, or "telegraph wire," for the first sign of dinner. The orb weaver must detect the presence of prey by touch, because her eyesight is extremely poor. At the first vibration she detects, she immediately tests the web for the size and location of her prey, very rapidly pluck-

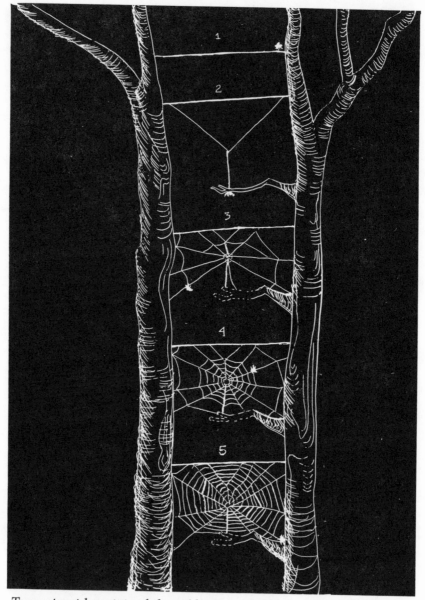

*To construct her state-of-the-spider-art web, the female orb weaver
(1) tosses out a thickened "bridge" line between two supports;
(2) drops down at the halfway point to form a triangle and plumb
line; (3) constructs the outermost frame of the orb; (4) weaves a
rough temporary dry spiral; and (5) removes the temporary dry spiral
and weaves a finely woven permanent sticky spiral.*

ing each spoke of the web before the prey can escape or damage the web. The tension in a line tells her just how large and how strong her prey is and how quickly she must act.

A young garden spider will often cut a large insect such as a bumblebee loose before the insect can damage the web or turn on its much smaller captor. A larger, more experienced spider, on the other hand, can quickly truss up a victim as large as a bumblebee. She speeds to the kill and swiftly spins a long length of fine silk around the insect as she revolves the bug with her legs, biting into it and injecting it with poison as she trusses it up. She then repairs the broken web threads and carries her mummified quarry back to the hub—taking care to move across only the dry spokes—where she hangs it from the underside of the web by a short thread for later consumption. She then returns to her post.

The orb web is the most highly refined of all aerial spiderwebs. Built on a slight slant, it passively screens the air night and day, netting the garden spider an extremely varied and well-balanced diet. Even though the orb web is virtually invisible even to small insects, it can withstand pressures of up to one thousand times the weight of its own designer. It is perfectly conceived to ensure the garden spider's safety while acting as a deadly net for airborne insects. Even tiny spiderlings can construct their own orb webs without any instruction, but the largest and most perfectly formed orb webs are built by practiced adult females. These virtual works of art can often be seen in the fall, when the garden spider has grown large after a long season of active web building and feasting.

SEVENTEEN

The Stickleback's Aquatic Nursery

T HE LITTLE BROOK STICKLEBACK *(EUCALIA INCONSTANS)*, A common fish of ponds and streams on both sides of the country, takes the duties and responsibilities of fatherhood, hearth, and home to unusual lengths. Unlike most fish, which choose makeshift locations to lay their eggs and more often than not abandon the eggs immediately after they are deposited, the male stickleback is so consumed by parental duties that he excludes the female stickleback from virtually all aspects of nesting and nurturing the young. While many other male fish are known to ferociously guard their eggs and offspring against intruders, none devotes as much time and energy as the male stickleback to constructing a safe haven for his eggs and fry as well as protecting them against the hazards of their watery environment.

In early spring, at the height of the stickleback's mating season, the male begins to feel the sure stirrings of fatherhood. His usual drab body color changes dramatically from a dull greenish gray to a vibrant red and blue. Even his eye color changes, from an indistinct brown to a brilliant emerald green. While casting about for suitable mothers for his unborn progeny, the male stickleback simultaneously begins to build the family abode. The male stickleback's dome-shaped nest, which will serve for breeding as well as raising the young from eggs to fry, is one of the most complicated nests built by any fish.

He begins by digging a neat, shallow crater in the bed of a pond or stream, often locating it near live, thick-stemmed vegetation, which he will later use to help bolster the walls of the above-ground structure. He then fills in the crater with sand and meticulously chewed-up plant roots and other fibrous debris to form a solid foundation for the shell of the nest as well as a cushioned cradle for the young. He "weaves" the nest's walls and roof out of fine plant stems, roots, and plant leaves, and then bores an entrance hole at one end of the nest.

Inside the roundish mound, the breeding and nesting space takes on a tubular shape roughly the size and contours of an adult stickleback. To keep the nest walls and roof from collapsing or breaking apart while mating with different females and during the several weeks of nurturing the eggs and the young, he "cements" the building materials together with a thick, gluelike secretion produced by a gland near his kidneys. This viscous nest-building material hardens upon contact with the water, so the male stickleback must work almost nonstop for as long as it takes to construct the nest, using his body and mouth to weave and shape the shell of the nest from the foundation up. Special efforts must be made to firmly anchor the walls to the foundation so the nest does not drift away in the current. The completed nest will resemble a small, shallow, slightly elongated dome or igloo resting flat on the ground.

The nest may take two to four days to complete, and the stickleback works on it almost around the clock, periodically taking a brief break to keep in touch with his first mate. These frequent visits with the mother of his future fry not only help to keep her near the nest site, but also seem to stimulate the flow of the gluelike material the male must constantly secrete while working on his nest and nursery.

There is frequent fierce competition among male sticklebacks both for available females and for the nest sites themselves. If another adult male stickleback shows up while the first is constructing his nest, the first male will have to pause in his nest building to fight off the intruder in order to protect both his mate and his home. Many fish reflect emotions such as aggression, fear, and triumph through a change in body behavior or coloration. The ultimate nest-building and breeding success of a male stickleback seems to be unerringly reflected in the vibrancy of his mating colors. The victor of such a battle will instantly become even brighter in color—which also stimulates the production of nest-building secretions—while the vanquished stickleback quickly grows dull again and loses all interest in mating as well as nest building.

When the nest is finished and the time finally arrives to mate, the female more often than not is reluctant to enter the nest, perhaps tired of waiting on the sidelines or rightly suspicious that she is, after all, incidental to the whole enterprise. If the male stickleback's chosen mate refuses to go into his nest and produce some eggs after all of his efforts, he simply forces her in by threatening her with his sharp back spines held erect

When the woven nest is finally completed, the female stickleback sometimes has to be forced by the male to enter the "nursery" and deposit her eggs.

and nipping at her tail fins with his jaws. Once the two stickle-backs mate, mother number one is not encouraged to linger. She bores a hole through the opposite end of the nest and exits immediately, completing the tunnel through the nest, which is now open at both ends. Two to five more mothers are then recruited by the male, relieved of their eggs, and discharged, until the stickleback has a cache of about eighty eggs to hoard and nurture.

While the eggs are incubating, the male stickleback must aerate them frequently. He does this by fanning a stream of water through the nest tunnel with his pectoral fins. He also busies himself by making constant repairs to the walls of the nest and standing guard, with his back spines erect, against other hungry males—and the mother sticklebacks themselves, which would, if given the opportunity, destroy the nest and eat

During breeding season, the male stickleback fish devotes a great deal of time to cultivating the affections of a female stickleback, but once he has her eggs, he chases her away from the nest.

*Once the right number of eggs have been deposited by several
females, the male stickleback becomes a doting father. He tirelessly
protects the eggs against other sticklebacks—including the mothers.
He aerates the eggs, and when the fry hatch and swim away,
he carries them back to the nest in his mouth.*

their own eggs. For four or more weeks the male actively guards his egg-filled nursery until the young sticklebacks are ready to hatch.

Once the eggs have hatched, the male stickleback's work begins in earnest. The young fry immediately dart out of the nest in all directions, and the father pursues them, catches them in his mouth, and spits them back into the nursery. The fry need constant surveillance; otherwise they will be swiftly swallowed by the waiting adult sticklebacks and other animals. Naturally, all during this time the father has little opportunity to forage for his own food. In fact, he eats so little and loses so much weight that when his progeny are finally large enough to leave the nest and fend for themselves, he often dies soon afterward from sheer exhaustion.

BIBLIOGRAPHY

Adler, Kraig, and Tim Halliday, editors. *The Encyclopedia of Reptiles and Amphibians.* New York: Facts on File, 1991.

Allaby, Michael. *Animal Artisans.* New York: Alfred A. Knopf, 1982.

Bateman, Graham, editor. *Encyclopedia of Birds.* Oxford, England: Equinox (Oxford), Ltd., 1985.

Behnke, Frances L. *A Natural History of Termites.* New York: Charles Scribner's Sons, 1977.

Blaney, Walter M. *How Insects Live.* New York: E. P. Dutton & Co., 1976.

Bonney, Rick. "Animal House: Think You're Warm and Cozy Inside That High Tech Tent? Try a Robin's Nest." *Backpacker* 14 (May 1986): 16–21.

Borror, Donald J., Dwight M. DeLong, and Charles A. Triplehorn. *An Introduction to the Study of Insects.* New York: Holt, Rinehart, and Winston, 1976.

Burton, John A., editor. *Owls of the World.* New York: E. P. Dutton & Co., 1973.

Caffin, Charles H. *How to Study Architecture.* New York: Tudor Publishing Co., 1937.

Chambers, Kenneth A. *A Country-Lover's Guide to Wildlife.* Baltimore: The Johns Hopkins University Press, 1979.

Chavin, Remy. *Animal Societies.* New York: Hill and Wang, 1968.

Collins, Nicholas E., and Elsie G. Collins. *Nest Building and Bird Behavior.* Princeton, NJ: Princeton University Press, 1984.

Costello, David F. *The World of the Ant.* New York: J. B. Lippincott Co., 1968.

Dumpert, K. *The Social Biology of Ants.* London: Pitman Publishing, Ltd., 1981.

Errington, Paul L. *Muskrat Populations.* Ames, IA: The Iowa State University Press, 1962.

Evans, Howard E., and Mary Jane West Eberhard. *The Wasps.* Ann Arbor, MI: The University of Michigan Press, 1966.

Feinstein, Harold. "Drawing on Nature: A New Generation of Engineers Explores the Design of Natural Forms and Discovers Evolution's Ideal Blueprints." *Audubon* 94 (May–June 1992): 76–81.

Forsyth, Adrian. *Mammals of the American North.* Ontario, Canada: Camden House Publishing, Ltd. 1985.

George, Jean Graighead. *Beastly Inventions.* New York: David McKay Company, 1970.

Gertsch, Willis J. *American Spiders.* New York: Van Nostrand Reinhold Co., 1979.

Hansell, Michael H. "Wasp Papier-Mâche: Most Often Respected for the Power of Their Sting, Many Wasps Are Masters of a Gentler Art." *Natural History* 98 (August 1989): 52–62.

Headstrom, Richard. *A Complete Field Guide to Nests in the United States.* New York: Ives Washburn, 1970.

Howse, Philip E. *Termites: A Study in Social Behavior.* London: Hutchinson University Library, 1960.

Hoyt, Murray. *The World of Bees.* New York: Coward McCann, 1965.

Jones, Dick. *Spider.* New York: Facts on File, 1986.

Kinkead, Eugene. *Squirrel Book.* New York: E. P. Dutton, 1980.

Krieger, Morris. *Homeowners' Encyclopedia of House Construction.* New York: McGraw-Hill, 1978.

Krombien, Karl V. *Trap-Nesting Wasps & Bees: Life Histories, Nests and Associates.* Washington, DC: Smithsonian Press, 1967.

Larson, Peggy Pickering, and Mervin W. Larson. *All about Ants.* New York: The World Publishing Co.

Leahy, Christopher. *The Birdwatcher's Companion.* Toronto, Canada: McGraw-Hill Ryerson, Ltd., 1982.

Lopez, Barry. *Arctic Dreams.* New York: Charles Scribner's Sons, 1986.

MacClintock, Dorcas. *A Natural History of Raccoons.* New York: Charles Scribner's Sons, 1981.

_____. *Squirrels of North America.* New York: Van Nostrand Reinhold Co., 1970.

McFarland, David. *The Oxford Companion to Animal Behavior.* New York: Oxford University Press, 1982.

McNamee, Thomas. *The Grizzly Bear.* New York: Alfred A. Knopf, 1984.

Mellanby, Kenneth. *The Mole.* New York: Taplinger Publishing Co., 1973.

Miles, Hugh. *The Track of the Wild Otter.* New York: St. Martin's Press, 1984.

Morris, Desmond. *Animalwatching.* New York: Crown Publishers, 1990.

Murie, Adolph. *The Grizzlies of Mount McKinley.* Washington, DC: U.S. Department of the Interior, National Park Service, 1981.

Orlando, Louise. "Decorating the Den." *Science World* 17 (Feb. 9, 1991): 9–11.

Palmer, Ralph S., editor. *Handbook of North American Birds,* Vol.5. New Haven, and London: Yale University Press, 1988.

Preston, Douglas J. "Nestworks." *Natural History* 91 (Sept. 1982): 80–83.

Preston-Mafham, Rod, and Ken Preston-Mafham. *Spiders of the World.* New York: Facts on File, 1984.

Risebero, Bill. *The Story of Western Architecture.* New York: Charles Scribner's Sons, 1979.

Rue, Leonard Lee. *Furbearing Animals of North America.* New York: Crown Publishers, 1981.

_____. *Pictorial Guide to the Mammals of North America.* New York: Thomas Y. Crowell Co., 1967.

Russell, Andy. *Grizzly Country.* New York: Nick Lyons Books, 1967.

Savage, Arthur, and Candace Savage. *Wild Mammals of Northwest America.* Baltimore: The Johns Hopkins University Press, 1981.

Stanek, V. J. *The Pictorial Encyclopedia of Insects.* London: The Hamlyn Publishing Group, Ltd., 1970.

Stokes, David, and Lillian Stokes. *Animal Tracking and Behavior.* Boston: Little, Brown and Co., 1986.

Stokes, Donald W. *A Guide to Bird Behavior,* Vol.2. Toronto, Canada: Little, Brown and Co., Ltd., 1983.

Sutton, Ann. *The Structure of Weaving.* Asheville, NC: Lark Books, 1982.

von Frisch, Karl. *Animal Architecture.* New York: Harcourt Brace Jovanovich, 1974.

Index